TALES OF
RACING AND
'CHASING

TALES OF RACING AND 'CHASING

Terry Biddlecombe
with Jeff Farmer

Illustrations by Jake Tebbit

To Bill.
Happy Birthday 1988.
From Minnie

STANLEY PAUL
London   Melbourne   Sydney   Auckland   Johannesburg

Stanley Paul & Co. Ltd

An imprint of Century Hutchinson Ltd

17–21 Conway Street, London W1P 6JD

Hutchinson Publishing Group (Australia) Pty Ltd
PO Box 496, Hawthorn, Melbourne, Victoria 3122

Hutchinson Group (NZ) Ltd
PO Box 40–086, Glenfield 10, Auckland

Hutchinson Group (SA) Pty Ltd
PO Box 337, Bergvlei 2012, South Africa

First published 1985

Set in Linoterm Century by
The Castlefield Press, Moulton, Northampton

Printed and bound in Great Britain by Anchor Brendon Ltd,
Tiptree, Essex

British Library Cataloguing in Publication Data

Biddlecombe, Terry
    Tales of racing and 'chasing.
    1. Horse-racing———— Anecdotes, facetiae, satire, etc.
    I. Title   II. Farmer, Jeff
    798.4 '0207   SF335.5

ISBN 0 09 162690 0

CONTENTS

FOREWORD

When I walked away from Cheltenham in March 1974 at the end of my career as a National Hunt jockey, I hardly realized what a void it would leave in my life.

Since then I have tried to fill the gap by retaining my contact with racing as a breeder; through my work as a television racing reporter and helping my wife Ann bring up the next generation of Biddlecombes – our sons Robert and James.

I have also found that friendships made in racing last a lifetime.

Chatting over old times with the likes of Mercy Rimell and Fred Winter, Mike Scudamore and David Nicholson; discussing more recent events with personalities like Jenny Pitman and John Francome has made compiling *Tales of Racing and 'Chasing* an enormous pleasure.

I hope it provides the reader with as much enjoyment.

Terry Biddlecombe

JOCKEYS

Soon after my retirement in 1974, the directors of Cheltenham Racecourse did me the honour of staging a Jockeys' Dinner – to bid farewell to Biddles, as it were. Came the day and, still feeling the withdrawal symptoms, I hadn't given a thought to my speech for the occasion. Josh Gifford, who was staying with me for a couple of days, offered his assistance. 'Don't worry, I'll write it for you – anyway I know about the presentation and you don't,' said Josh. I suppose I should have known better, but I left it to Josh, and as we arrived at Cheltenham for the dinner he slipped my script into my pocket. After much wine, a superb meal and generous servings of port, I was presented with a beautiful set of Snaffles racing prints.

It had been an emotional night, and when I staggered to my feet I was grateful that Josh had taken the time to mark my card for the speech. I carefully unfolded his script, focused as clearly as I could and started reading: 'Directors of Cheltenham Racecourse, fellow jockeys, good friends, my sincere thanks for a wonderful evening . . .' (This is good, I thought. For once in his life, Gifford has done me a favour.) I continued: 'It's not a night for long speeches, so I'd just like to thank everyone for this super set of Snaffles prints – I'm sure they'll look lovely hung in the cowshed . . .'

COWSHED? I murmured something like 'Oh bollocks' to myself – or it might have been audible. Somewhere in the distance I could hear Gifford chuckling, but I sensed that not too many of the other guests were joining him. My embarrassment was deep – but it always helps to know you are not the only victim. I heard later that Agostini, the former world motor-cycling champion, had fallen for a similar practical joke. Agostini could hardly speak a word of English, so the late Mike Hailwood offered to write his thank-you speech for the dinner to celebrate his world-championship victory. Just as trusting as I'd been at Cheltenham, Agostini rose to his feet, opened his script and, so the story goes, said: 'Ladeez and gentermen . . . well, fucka my old boots.'

My first winner was at Wincanton on 6 March 1958 when I rode the 20-1 outsider Burnella to beat Fred Winter on Piper, the 4-7 favourite, by a head. I hadn't got a clue whether I'd won as we rode towards the unsaddling enclosure – an unknown seventeen-year-old amateur alongside the champion jockey. So, respectfully, I asked Mr Winter: 'Did I win, sir?' Fred, who has been known to swear at odd times in the heat of the moment, stared at me coldly and replied: 'How the bloody hell should I know?'

It was my first glimpse of Fred's famed competitive spirit, something I always admired and tried to emulate. He hated being beaten, and even made the lads in the weighing room cough up after his first Grand National ride on the no-hoper Glenfire in 1951. The senior jockeys bet the up-and-coming Winter that he wouldn't get past Becher's first time round. Fred won the money. He negotiated Becher's safely, then fell two fences later at the Canal Turn and walked home to collect.

Since that first day at Wincanton, Fred has never lost the nack of putting me in my place. As recently as the start of the 1984-5 jumping season, I was interviewing Fred on the subject of National Hunt jockeys. 'Who's the best?' I asked him. 'I think Johnny Francome is the best I've ever seen,' he said, adding, with a wicked glint in his eye, 'Oh, sorry, Terry, I forgot I was talking to you.'

Fred Winter was at the top of his profession when he was offered the job of first jockey to Fulke Walwyn's stable in 1962, so Fred could afford to impose certain conditions before accepting the position. 'I won't school novice chasers, and I won't ride over fences at Leicester or Plumpton,' he told Fulke. That agreed, Fred soon got cracking and rode Burton Tan to a comfortable win in a chase at Devon and Exeter. The following week, Burton Tan was in at Plumpton and Fulke asked Fred to ride the horse again. 'Not me,' said Fred. 'He got you round at Devon and Exeter,' Fulke protested – but it made no difference. So Dave Dick took over the ride on Burton Tan at Plumpton, fell, and broke his collar bone.

Nor did Fred do Dave Dick any favours in a twenty-two horse novice chase at Wye. It was so narrow going to the first fence that a twenty-two-horse field was asking for trouble, but Fred jumped off well and got a good position up the rail. Just as he came to the first, Fred heard Dave screaming behind him: 'Fred, Fred – give me some light.' 'No way,' shouted Fred, and as he jumped the fence safely, he saw Dave Dick going sideways and jumping the first on the hurdle course.

In sixteen years of National Hunt race-riding, I had some odd, controversial and occasionally ridiculous exchanges with my fellow jockeys between the tapes and the winning post. I have stolen whips from beaten jockeys after I'd lost mine – and I once even showed the courtesy to offer a tenner for a whip on the way to the second last. The offer was refused, and I was so steamed up about it I went to and won anyway.

I 'accidentally' hit the great Persian War across the head with my whip, when Jimmy Uttley tried to force him through a non-existent gap at the last before I won the inaugural Irish Sweeps Hurdle on Normandy in 1969. I had to give Josh Gifford two sharp cracks during the 1963 Grand National. He had just fallen on Out and About and I couldn't resist a snigger as I went past my stranded pal. In the heat of the moment, Josh decided that it was about time I parted company with Loyal Tan. As we plodded past him, Josh caught hold of my leg and hung on as if he were hitching a lift back to the finish. My pleas to let go fell on deaf ears, so there was only one thing for it. I gave Josh two swift reminders with my stick and Loyal Tan continued his journey unhindered.

Most jockeys who have ridden round Aintree will have a similar bizarre tale to tell, and we've all had our share of being 'done' or being helped back into the saddle. But I believe that Fred Winter and I share the distinction of being the only two jockeys to shake hands during a race. It was Fred's last day as a jockey and my last chance to ride against one of the greatest of all time. The race was at Cheltenham and we were upsides until we jumped the water, when I realized mine was going better than his. I reached over towards Fred, shook his hand and said: 'I've got to leave you now, mate, but I can't go without saying what a pleasure it's been riding with a real gent.'

When The Reject catapulted John Francome into retirement at Chepstow on 9 April 1985, he celebrated the end of a spectacular riding career in a way only jockeys would fully appreciate. I telephoned John at his Lambourn home just after he had got back from Chepstow, bruised and limping from the fall he had decided would be his last. There were no tears, no emotion. 'I've started celebrating already, Bidders,' he told me. 'I'm sitting here with a big bacon sandwich and a bottle of champagne – and I know I can do the same thing again tomorrow morning if I feel like it.'

After weeks of richly deserved tributes to the most successful jump jockey of all time, there was no deflecting John from a retirement decision many thought premature. 'Are you missing it?' I asked him, 'Yes – like earache. You

know what, I wouldn't come back – not even if somebody offered me the ride on Pegasus.'

We did see John in the saddle once more, when he took on Lester Piggott in a challenge match over one and threequarter miles on the flat at Warwick, and in the paddock before the race he showed he had lost none of his dry sense of humour during the early weeks of his new career as a trainer. Francome was asked by an interviewer how he thought the race would go. 'Can't really say,' he replied, 'but whatever beats me will win it.'

Much as it will annoy him, I would like to put into print for the first time that Paul Kellaway did not out-ride me to win the 1969 Cheltenham Gold Cup on What A Myth. I was on Domacorn, owned by Bryan Jenks and trained by Fred Rimell, and it was the most exasperating race of my career. I felt I had a vested interest in Domacorn. I'd recommended him to Mr Jenks and had won on him at Ascot, Newbury and Chepstow. He was a big, leggy horse who demanded your maximum attention and effort. You couldn't even have a chat with the other jockeys on the way round or he became unbalanced. But I was pretty sure I'd got to the bottom of him by the time we took on the Gold Cup field. Coming down the hill I felt that we only had to stand up to win, and as we approached the second last, What A Myth was the only, if remote, danger.

However Domacorn decided to walk through the fence and I lost my stick. For years I'd performed conjuring tricks to retrieve seemingly lost whips, but not this time. As I grabbed frantically at thin air, Paul went past me laughing out loud. I couldn't even beg, buy or borrow another jockey's whip – something I'd done to winning effect in the past – because no one else was near us. So as Kellaway strode away I was stranded. I knew the big horse needed a couple of reminders to go on and win his race, but all I could do was sit there and slap him with my hand. Paul beat me by a length-and-a-half. If it's any consolation for anyone who backed Domacorn, I'd have won a hundred yards with my stick.

The rear of the field in a three-mile novices chase can be the loneliest place in National Hunt racing. I was there at Wincanton one day and I had never felt lonelier, but you have to keep going. Gradually the horse in front of me began to tire and I was looking forward to some company. At least we could have a natter as we both plodded home tailed off. We took the next fence upsides, but before I could start a conservation the other horse did a somersault and his jockey landed on the back of mine. Every jockey tries to grab something when he falls, but this was ridiculous. My horse was slow enough with one jockey on his back – so it was one shove and my uninvited partner was off again.

Jimmy Lindley, now an expert paddock summarizer on BBC television, was an exceptional flat-racing jockey, winning many of the top races, but Jimmy began his career riding over the hurdles. He won thirty-six National Hunt races and finished third in the 1958 Champion Hurdle on Retour de Flamme. Jimmy and I have been good friends for years – ever since our first meeting at the start of a novices hurdle at the old Birmingham track in December 1959.

I was still a young, unknown amateur and I was probably looking a bit nervous when I arrived at the gate on Birinkiana, trained by Bill Wilesmith from Worcester. Jimmy walked his mount across towards me and said: 'Follow me, lad. I'll give you a lead.' Jimmy already had the reputation of being a fine rider, so I was delighted to accept his invitation – until we reached the first hurdle.

I thought all I had to do was to follow him round to keep out of trouble, but Jimmy, riding a horse called Mosterton, slipped up approaching the first and although he scrambled over it, I crashed through the hurdle after meeting it blind. When we got to the second, Mosterton tried to refuse and again the last place on earth you wanted to be was behind him. I decided it was time to forget Jimmy's kind offer and make my own way home. I jumped past Mosterton and eventually finished way down the field – but a long way in front of Jimmy, who finished last.

A few years after I retired as a jockey, the BBC television sports unit asked me if I would ride over three fences of the Grand National course in the company of Jimmy Hill for a preview of Aintree's big meeting. I knew that Jimmy, in addition to his talent as a football administrator and television presenter, was an experienced rider in the hunting field and had been taught by a hard taskmaster in Ted Edgar, the international showjumper. I must admit that I wasn't looking forward to it. I hadn't ridden over racecourse fences for ages, I'd put on too much weight and I've never regarded Aintree as a place to play around. But when we got to Liverpool, Jimmy was confident enough, so we put on racing colours to look the part and they brought out our horses.

On the way to the start, I told Jimmy that the secret was to make sure we didn't go too fast into the first fence. We had to keep our mounts under complete control, I insisted. Just as I was giving these instructions, Jimmy's horse broke into a trot, then moved up to a canter and suddenly they were galloping away from me in the direction of the stables. Jimmy eventually pulled up, and when he returned to our starting point he was noticeably less concerned than me about the task ahead of us.

'Are you okay,' I enquired. 'Yes, mate, let's go,' said Jimmy. So off we went. We approached the first at a nice, moderate pace and both negotiated it safely. 'How was that Jimmy?' I shouted across. No answer was forthcoming. I thought it was time to give Jimmy a little confidence booster by taking his mind off the problems of the second fence. 'The one *after* this is the one to worry about,' I advised. 'Right,' replied Jimmy, with grim determination. A similar psychological trick had worked for me the first time I rode in the Grand National on Aliform in 1960. On the way round, I'd asked Taffy Jenkins: 'Which one's Becher's?' He lied: 'It's the fence after this one.' I'd jumped Becher's Brook without even thinking about it.

But the ruse didn't work quite as well for Jimmy Hill. He jumped our second fence, but as we landed his horse stumbled. Jimmy's mount lost an iron and he then came swerving straight across the course in front of me, shouting: 'I've pulled my bloody hamstring.' They tell me that a pulled hamstring is a common football injury, but you don't often hear of it happening jumping a fence. We never did reach the third, and I was delighted to get away in one piece. Back in the weighing room we unwound with a few drinks, and they must have done Jimmy and his hamstring the world of good. By the time we left Aintree, he was seen to be walking very sound.

My weekly racing feature for Central Television's Friday evening *Central Sport* programme has helped me remain closely involved with both National Hunt and the flat. The co-operation I've received has been immense, and I like to think that the filming with the Central team has taken millions of armchair racing fans behind-the-scenes. What they don't get to see are what television people call the 'out-takes' – all the clangers and cock-ups, the giggles, the pregnant silences and the stray expletives. Dennis Norden makes a hit television show out of them, so now I'll present the Biddlecombe version of *It'll Be Alright on the Night*.

The starring role has to go to Willie Carson. He's brilliant to interview – once he lets you start. I normally interview Willie at his home near Cirencester before the start of the flat season. He always looks bronzed and fit after a winter riding or holidaying in the sun – and he's invariably in a devilish mood. I used to start the interview with a question about Willie's tour during the winter – but not any more because he put paid to that one last year.

'Well, Willie, you've just spent most of the winter riding in the sun in America, South Africa, Australia and Hong Kong – are you looking forward to the new season at home?' 'Terry, why is it that every year you start off by asking me the same bloody question.' CUT!

The film crew wait in gleeful anticipation these days to see what new show-stopper Willie has waiting for me. This year he produced one of his best. I'd learned my lesson about the winter tour, so I set off on a different tack. 'Right, Willie, it's the first big handicap of the new season on Saturday – how do you fancy your chances in the Lincoln?' Carson stays stone-faced – and silent.

I go again, rephrasing the question. 'Well, Willie you're on the favourite in the Lincoln on Saturday – what are his chances?' Carson remains tight-lipped but he starts inching forward towards me – then he suddenly bends and bites the foam-rubber cap off the microphone. CUT!

John Francome must have been taking lessons from Willie Carson when I interviewed him before the start of his last season as a jockey. We filmed a feature on the tennis court at my home, and I have to admit that the set we played was so one-sided I hardly won a point. We then arranged that at the end of the interview, I'd wish John all the best for the new National Hunt season and he'd respond by wishing me well with the tips I give for 'Terry's Treble' on the *Central Sport* programme.

'Thanks for the game, John – and be lucky in the new season.' 'Thanks, Terry, but I have to say that your tennis is almost as bad as your tips.' We both collapsed, and perhaps I should have realized then that we hadn't been asked to do the pay-off lines again. By the time the piece got on the air, the out-take had become an in-take!

10

Lester Piggott is not only a mate of mine; he's also my idol among flat jockeys. He's the greatest of all time but as everyone knows he's a man of few words – and he's virtually monosyllabic if you catch him in the wrong mood. I was filming Henry Cecil's string at work on Newmarket Heath for my television spot just after Piggott's well-publicized split with the leading French owner Daniel Wildenstein, who had decreed that Lester would ride no more of his horses on the racecourse.

This particular morning Lester worked a horse who was doing a fair impression of Pegasus – and never came off the bit. As he dismounted, I ventured the opinion that the animal looked impressive. 'Bloody useless,' said Lester and stomped off towards his Mercedes. Three days later a colt made his racecourse debut at Doncaster and won doing handstands. It was Claude Monet – owned by D. Wildenstein, ridden by P. Eddery. Now, I'm not a seasoned Newmarket work-watcher, but I'd swear it was the same horse!

Lester rode one of the races of his life to win the Grand Prix de Saint-Cloud in July 1984 on Teenoso, which had won the Epsom Derby for Geoffrey Wragg a year earlier. Lester had a badly cut eye because Teenoso had reared up during the parade before the race, but despite the pain, he cantered off to the start determined that nothing was going to deprive him of the chance to win one of Europe's best races, worth £82,000. By the time the field had reached the straight and Lester was about to deliver his challenge on Teenoso, the blood from the cut eye had virtually filled up his goggles, but through the red mists Lester rode one of his typical finishes to get up and win by a head.

Lester lost so much blood he could hardly stand up after the race, and you may remember seeing some graphic newspaper photographs of his blood-streaked face and colours. As is often the case in France, they gave trophies to the winning owner and trainer, and for this race there were exquisite china plates. Back at the airport, everyone in the Teenoso party was reviewing the spoils of a successful day at Saint-Cloud. Then someone asked Lester, still ashen-faced and in obvious discomfort from his injured eye, 'Did you get anything?' 'Yes,' said Lester with that familiar deadpan expression, 'they gave me the *Croix de Guerre*.'

Not many trainers had the nerve to confront Lester Piggott with a tirade of criticism when was beaten on one of their horses, but a few years ago, the Lambourn trainer Ben Leigh went for Lester with both barrels in the unsaddling enclosure. Ben said his piece in no uncertain manner and concluded: 'What's more, you'll never ride for me again.' Lester looked him up and down, po-faced, and replied: 'I'd better give up then.'

Just as succinct was the advice offered by Lester to Beckhampton trainer Jeremy Tree in the paddock at Salisbury. Jeremy told Lester that he'd promised to go to a girls' school and give them a talk on racing. 'What can I tell them?' he asked. 'Tell them you've got flu,' replied Lester.

There were bound to be some problems breaking through the language barrier when the top National Hunt jockeys from around the world assembled at Cheltenham for the first World Jockeys' Championship in April 1984. Interpreters were available – but could they really grasp the full meaning of a trainer's instructions and transmit them correctly to the jockey? In the case of the Italian champion Giannantonio Colleo, there was a definite breakdown in communications.

Colleo rode Misty Dale for Ross-on-Wye trainer John Edwards. Through an interpreter in the paddock, John – whose Italian is marginally worse than Colleo's non-existent English – instructed the jockey to keep the horse handy and never be far off the pace. So John was mortified to see his horse dropped out at the rear of the field and then brought with a late run which turned out to be too late. 'It's a good job we couldn't understand each other afterwards,' John confided. The story goes that the interpreter had been borrowed from a local Italian restaurant, so it was probably a case of ordering spaghetti and getting canneloni.

Shinobu Hoshino is a jockey few of us had ever heard of before the first National Hunt World Jockeys' Championship at Cheltenham in April 1984. But in the very first race, the tiny Japanese rider streaked clear from the last to win in a canter on Fulke Walwyn's hurdler Desert Hero. It was the cause of much celebration. I was watching from the balcony of the National Hunt Room with the championship organizers Bob Champion and Bev Walker and as Shinobu cleared the last, we might have been in the middle of Tokyo.

Shinobu's missus was shouting him home – all four feet six of her bouncing up and down, and even the previously inscrutable representative of the Japanese Jockey Club was screaming his head off in his native tongue. I doubt whether the hallowed steps of the Cheltenham grandstand had ever heard anything quite like it, and there was more to come in the winner's enclosure. As Shinobu came in, looking like an Oriental Willie Carson perched on top of a horse built to carry twelve stone, Fulke Walwyn had one of the biggest smiles I've ever seen. Shinobu is about eight stone wringing wet and Fulke was towering above him. They couldn't understand a word they were saying to each other, but a winner is a winner in any language.

When Shinobu returned to England for the 1985 championship, I fixed him up to ride out and jump a few schooling fences at Sally Oliver's stable at Suckley in Worcestershire. Being an excellent hostess and a creative cook, Sally phone the Japanese Embassy in London to find out what she should offer the jockey and his entourage for breakfast. In Japan, she was told, it was customary for the jockey to be served rice with miso soup. The rice was no problem – but miso soup? Sally must have tried every food store and supermarket within thirty miles to find the ingredients for the recommended Japanese breakfast – but no success. 'Give him bacon and eggs,' I suggested – and left her to it.

Shinobu arrived at Suckley by Rolls Royce and rode out resplendent in purple silks – with his name in Japanese hieroglyphics emblazoned on the back – wafer-thin red boots and pink gloves. I thought he was going to a fancy-dress party – but once he sits on a horse he immediately commands your respect. He cantered up and down the all-weather gallop on one of Sally's horses, Courting Boy, then popped him impressively over the schooling fences. It was time for breakfast, and as we walked back to the house I wondered how Sally had solved her catering dilemma. As soon as I got through the door, my nose gave me the answer. Shinobu was greeted by a veritable feast – the traditional English breakfast. Sizzling bacon and eggs,

huge pork sausages, tomatoes, baked beans, sweetbreads, mushrooms and fried bread. And he tucked into the lot with great relish. 'He'll have trouble making ten stone tomorrow,' said Sally's husband, Henry.

Shinobu made the weight alright at Cheltenham the following day, but the horses he drew in his three legs of the championship were so moderate, he might as well have stayed in Tokyo. I was beginning to feel sorry for him when someone told me that riding about sixty horses a season in Japan earned him the best part of £400,000. It made me think seriously about losing four stone, making a comeback and heading east with a lightweight saddle.

Before the 1984 championship, I drove over to David Nicholson's gallops at Condicote near Stow-on-the-Wold to watch the Russian jockey Yusei Kaseev. As David's string was ready to pull out at seven o'clock, the village green at Condicote must have resembled a scene from a James Bond film. Comrade Kaseev and another Russian jockey were given a leg up, David was playing 007 supervising his first lot, Central Television were filming it – the whole scene watched over by a stern-looking gentleman in the inevitable black leather coat.

The Russians rode well and skipped their mounts over a couple of schooling hurdles. Just as we were about to head back to the yard, the man in the black leather coat opened up what I thought was a binocular case – and produced a bottle of vodka. 'In Russia after the good gallop, we drink the health of the horses and riders,' said the interpreter as David was presented with a bottle of 100 per cent proof. 'I'm afraid it's a shade too early for me,' said David, 'but I'm sure Biddles will try it.' I opened the bottle, said 'cheers' all round, and took a sizeable swig just to show these Russians what we are made of. It blew my bloody head off. And, as I stood there gasping for breath, the man in the black leather coat smiled for the first time that morning.

Michael Scudamore, my great pal and mentor, was called up for his National Service at the peak of his riding career – and it only cost him three winners. Twenty-six days into his Army service with the Royal Horse Artillery, Scu was bemoaning the fact that Bryan Marshall had replaced him on a winning treble at the Aintree meeting, when he was discharged with feet unsuitable to march for Queen and country.

Scu's bad feet were a weighing-room legend, but he reckons they saved his career as a jockey. That month in the Army saw his weight increase from ten stone three pounds to eleven stone five pounds. He had several operations on his feet – and one near-operation at the hands of Stan Mellor. At a cocktail party thrown by David Nicholson, Stan decided to try out a new lawn mower. He lost control of it, ran over Scu's right foot and tore off the top of his shoe. Scu looked down, counted his toes and laughed like a drain – which was typical of the man.

He used to say: 'The three greatest thrills in life are riding round Aintree, taking a parachute jump – and you know the other one.' One thrill he failed to mention was riding a chaser called Greektown, who was trained by Willie Stephenson, for whom Michael won the Grand National on Oxo in 1959. Scu would tell me: 'This horse is so free that you get as far as the "Oh" in "Oh shit" and he's through the fence and away.' Before schooling Greektown one day, Scu asked Willie Stephenson: 'Can I have breakfast before I go out?' 'Why?' asked Willie. 'I might not come back after schooling this bugger.'

18

Michael Scudamore was looking forward to a quiet day at home when Lambourn trainer Geoffrey Kennedy rang him and requested his services to ride a novice chaser at Leicester. 'No, thank you,' said Scu, but Geoffrey talked him into it. Scu began to suspect he was in for a difficult ride when he reached Leicester, saw that only four ran in the novices chase and there was no shortage of available jockeys at the track. He decided to look for a quiet run round the outside, but after a couple of fences Tim Molony came charging upsides on a great big horse, with a tube in his throat, a martingale and his head in the air.

'Where the bloody hell are you going?' asked Scu. 'It looks like I'm going on,' said Tim. 'Okay, I'll come with you.' Scu fell at the next, Tim at the fence after that. As they met between fences, Tim said: 'Come on, let's go back and see if there are any spares in the next race.'

Arthur (A.P.) Thompson used to sit in the weighing-room before a race with a broad grin on his face. One day Michael Scudamore asked him why he was always smiling before going out. 'I'm thinking of you silly buggers chasing round behind me,' said Arthur. Arthur had one way of riding, and it was from the front. On the right horse up north, he was virtually unbeatable.

Scu used to say that Arthur would get a couple of the younger riders closest to him to give him a running commentary of what was going on behind. Scu and some of the lads got wise to this, and he delights in recalling the day when he came up behind Thompson's mount and shouted: 'Watch your inner, Arthur.' Arthur pulled across to find nobody there, and Scu ran straight on to beat him.

Arthur Freeman was not so lucky at Southwell one day, when he tried to steal up Thompson's inner. He just reached across and snatched the bridle off Freeman's horse.

The highlights of Arthur Thompson's fine National Hunt career came at Aintree, where he rode Sheila's Cottage to win the 1948 Grand National and made it a double with Teal in 1952 – both horses trained by Neville Crump. Away from Aintree, though Arthur's speciality was winning from the front, and although he was based in the North, his name popped up in a heated discussion at Fulke Walwyn's Lambourn stable one evening.

Fulke trained the impressive chaser Mont Tremblant for Dorothy Paget, and Bryan Marshall had been instructed to ride a waiting race on the horse at

Cheltenham. Fulke's orders were to hold him up until the second last, but Bryan had tried to make all the running and got beaten. Both Fulke and Dorothy Paget were furious, and Bryan thought he'd better call on his trainer when he returned to Lambourn that evening. When Bryan arrived, Fulke was in the kitchen, carving himself a lump of cheese. He greeted his jockey by slamming the cheese knife into the kitchen table and booming: 'If I want Arthur Thompson to ride for me, I'll bloody well book him.'

At less fraught times, Bryan would telephone Fulke in the evening to report on how his mounts for the stable had run during the afternoon. Bryan had a habit of going through the races fence by fence, and if he'd had five rides it could be quite a time-consuming business. Fulke, who always preferred tending his horses to talking to jockeys, eventually found a way of editing Bryan's reports. Whenever the jockey rang with his daily summary, Fulke would tell him: 'Just skip the first mile-and-a-half.'

The Bollinger racing awards dinner in London was always one of the highlights of my year as a jockey – and the standard of hospitality was such that it was an achievement to leave there sober. Few, however, have made a more unusual trip home from the Bollinger than Macer Gifford. It was just after the breathalyser appeared on the scene so Macer, sensibly, decided to take the train. He got to London alright and enjoyed the dinner. Then things started to go wrong.

First Macer lost all his money in a brief but disastrous visit to the gaming tables – but at least he had his return ticket for the midnight train back home to Huntingdon. He got to the station O.K. and boarded his train. The next thing he knew was that it was 5 a.m. and he was waking up in Newcastle-on-Tyne. With a dreadful hangover and no money, he began the long trek home – hitching a lift down the A1. Macer, one of the bravest men I knew, took it all in his stride. His only complaint: 'I missed a good day's shooting.'

'Frenchie' Nicholson rode a horse at Fontwell one day which he thought could win but he had been told by the trainer that it was 'officially' not fancied. 'I'm going to jump off and make all,' said Frenchie. 'It will blow up,' said the trainer. Frenchie duly jumped off, made all and won comfortably. Back in the winner's enclosure, the trainer told Frenchie: 'You're getting the sack.' Said Frenchie: 'Well my sack is full – I hope yours is!'

A few years later, when Frenchie was proving just as successful training horses as he was riding them, he found an unusual way of 'improving' a horse he wanted to sell. It was called Côte D'Azur, and Frenchie rode it at Wincanton before they had rails around the track. When the field vanished into the fog over the back straight Frenchie took a short cut across the middle of the course, and when they came back into view Côte D'Azur finished a creditable fifth. After the race Bob Turnell was asked by his trainer how on earth Frenchie had finished in front of his horse. 'You should have seen where he went,' said Bob.

Tim Brookshaw, one of the hardest and bravest jockeys I ever had the privilege to ride with, had his own personal hallmark – the blood-curdling scream he would let out if he was approaching the last with a chance. The young Josh Gifford felt the full impact of it one day when he came to the last hurdle in a race at Birmingham looking all over a winner. The 'Brown Cow' – as we all called Tim – was Josh's only challenger and he loomed upsides, swinging his whip like a shillelagh in his right hand and screaming at his horse: 'Go on, you old bugger.'

I could hear it almost fifty yards away and Josh, hearing the Brookshaw war cry at close quarters for the first time, was so surprised he took off too soon. The effort needed from Josh to get his mount over the hurdle was so demanding that he swallowed his false teeth. As he took off up the run-in, the dental plate he'd had fitted to replace teeth knocked out in an earlier accident got stuck in his throat. Josh, spluttering and half-choking by now, lost his momentum as he struggled to retrieve his teeth from his gullet and the wily old 'Brown Cow' got up on the line to win by a head.

Jeff King, a superb jockey and now an up-and-coming trainer, won many top races during his riding career but, like me, never managed to win a Grand National. Yet Jeff will tell you that one of his greatest races was to finish third in the 1969 National on Bob Turnell's Rondetto. Jeff was riding with probably the worst black eye I have ever seen. He collected it when he fell in the Topham, and during the forty-eight hours before the National it came up like a huge black egg.

At Aintree you need eyes in the back of your head, and to ride round there half-blind is some achievement. Jeff managed it by lifting and cocking his head to give his good eye a sight of every fence, but it must have been like riding round in blinkers and an eyepatch. If it had taken Jeff and Rondetto an hour to get round four-and-a-half miles of Aintree in one piece, I would have been there waiting to applaud. For them to finish in the frame left me speechless.

Everyone hopes to make a good impression on the first day of a new job, but few can have got off to a worse start than Nigel Twiston-Davies on his first Monday morning as a new employee of the Rimell stable. Twist – who became an accomplished amateur rider and is now training – did not have the best of preparations. He spent Sunday playing cricket with a team of jockeys, and after the game fell into the clutches of two other Rimell hands, Sam Morshead and Kim Bailey, for a few drinks.

Come seven o'clock Monday morning Twist was not feeling at his best, but as the Kinnersley string was due to pull out for exercise, he was given a leg up and all he could do was hope for an easy morning, merging into the background. But it's tradition at Kinnersley that a newcomer is left at the tail-end of the string, so that Mercy Rimell can have a chat and get to know him.

As Twist's raging headache began to develop into waves of nausea, all he needed was to be in the company of the lady gaffer. He tried manfully to keep the conversation at an intelligent level and hoped that Mercy wouldn't notice him turning slowly green. But eventually Twist reached the point of no return – he knew he was going to be sick. 'Do excuse me, madam,' he spluttered. He turned away feigning a coughing fit, removed his helmet and . . . well, I'll leave the rest to your imagination. Suffice it to say that Twist bought a new helmet that afternoon.

Sammy Millbanks rode for many years out of Lambourn and was always one of the great characters around the busy racing village. At Bath one day, Sammy rode a horse for Fulke Walwyn. It was strongly fancied, but in the hue and cry of the race the horse was ridden contrary to the trainer's instructions and was a fast-finishing fourth. Fulke is not a man to mince words when a horse he thinks should have won ends up out of the frame – as I found out myself on occasion. So Sammy had to stand there after the race while Fulke delivered a major bollocking. When Fulke finally concluded, Sammy managed to get a word in. 'Never mind, guvnor,' he said, 'sometimes I'm brilliant.'

Sammy was rarely stuck for a one-liner, but even he was left speechless after a horse had bolted with him at Lingfield. They went three times round the track and ended through the rails, finally coming to a halt in the members' car park. When the trainer caught them up, Sammy said: 'Sorry, sir, I couldn't hold one side of him.' 'I see,' said the trainer mystified. 'Which side was that?' Exit Sammy, shaking his head.

Lads get quite attached to their horses. They care for them day in, day out and can often show their disappointment when a jockey fails to live up to their expectations on race day. After I'd finished second on a horse trained by Bill Denton at Cheltenham – thinking I'd done well to get that close – his head lad asked me: 'Did you get paid for riding that race? I could have done better blindfolded.'

A Lambourn lad was even more disrespectful when a well-known New-market jockey, who wore a deaf aid, dismounted after being beaten on his favourite filly. 'I could do nothing with her. She's a cow,' said the jockey. 'Shut up and get away from her, you battery-driven bugger,' came the reply.

Speaking of lads, early in my career I rode in the same race as my father several times – and only once did he do me a favour. It was at Worcester and I came up behind him full of running. 'Get over, you old bugger,' I shouted. To my surprise, Dad pulled over, let me through the inner and gave me the chance to go on and win. I went over to thank him afterwards and he promptly told me: 'If your name hadn't been Biddlecombe, I'd have done you good and proper there, you cheeky little sod.'

On another occasion Dad was riding in a race at Chepstow, and as he was walking his mount round the paddock, this fellow leaning against the rails shouted: 'Eh Walt – I wouldn't ride that. I'd shoot it.' Not knowing what he meant, Dad went down to the start and prepared to line up. Suddenly the horse dived sideways, tried to bite the horse next to him and then caught hold of jockey Jack Dowdeswell's leg.

Jack eventually shook himself free and the field set off. Down the back straight, Dad thought his horse needed a couple of reminders to sort himself out, but after two sharp cracks with the whip, the horse turned round and tried to savage him. Dad wisely declared it a lost cause. He patted the horse down the neck and whispered: 'I think we'll go home quietly.'

Jeff Scudamore was the first generation of that famous riding family – father of Michael, grandfather of Peter. During his military service in the RAF Jeff was stationed at Bridlington, and noone was allowed to travel further than ten miles from camp. One Saturday Jeff couldn't resist breaking the ten-mile limit to go to Wetherby Races. Halfway through the meeting he was picked up by the Military Police and returned to base.

On Monday morning Jeff appeared before his commanding officer on a charge, and the conversation went something like this:

'Were you at Wetherby Races?'

'Yes, sir.'

'Did you back any winners?'

'No, sir.'

'Neither did I. Case dismissed.'

I was taking a day off from riding to go hunting at Ledbury and Josh Gifford, who had stayed overnight, decided to join me instead of going back to Ryan Price's stable at Findon to 'do his three'. We had a good day except for Josh getting a ticking off for heading the Master of the Hunt. But he knew there was worse to come when he returned to Findon the following day. 'Where the hell have you been?' demanded Ryan. 'Sorry, gaffer, I was delayed and couldn't get back.'

Josh spent most of the next week getting back into favour with Ryan when suddenly his little lie was exposed. Sitting on Ryan Price's desk was the new issue of *The Field* – opened at the page carrying a large photograph of Biddlecombe and Gifford out with the Ledbury Hunt.

If you have to ride novice chasers – and unfortunately it's an occupational hazard for jump jockeys – the last thing you want to do is remount after a fall. At Warwick one day, there were only two others left standing when I fell at the third last in a three-mile novices chase. I lay there winded and praying that the horse had gone away, but as I struggled to my feet, this dear little man in a St John's Ambulance uniform appeared – leading my horse back to me. 'Come on, matey,' he said, 'I'll give you a leg up. I've had a few bob each way on you and you can still finish third.' The St John's men do a great job on racecourses, so I resisted the temptation to tell him what to do with his each-way bet. 'Do me a favour,' I pleaded instead. 'Let him go, I think I've broken my collar bone.' So we went our separate ways – and I recovered from the 'broken collar bone' just in time to ride in the next race.

The only other time I've feigned injury was on a bitterly cold day at Hereford. I fell at the second last and went out like a light. Just as I was coming round, I heard someone say: 'It looks like he needs some more brandy.' So I closed my eyes again – and sipped.

I have a 100 per cent record in point-to-points. One ride, one winner. But I have to admit it was a dead-heat and it was achieved in painful circumstances.

I had already ridden under rules and had a couple of winners when I was invited to ride at Upton-on-Severn Point-to-Point. I bought new breeches and boots for the occasion and went there thinking I was Jack the Lad. My mount was fancied, and when I looked around the paddock at the older riders, I cockily thought: 'I'll ride this lot to sleep.' I was riding a horse called Holt Castle and I was so sure of myself, I spent most of the race trying to poke up the inside.

But at every bend I was absolutely crucified, and the experienced riders thought it was hilarious. When I finally got a run, I managed to get up and force a dead-heat. When I came back, my legs were black and blue. The new breeches were torn, the new boots were ripped. I never rode in another point-to-point.

You meet some crazy characters on the racing scene, but the craziest I ever met was on his way to a point-to-point. I was driving from Gloucester to Tewkesbury when I noticed a group of people standing round a reclining figure on the grass verge. I stopped, thinking there had been an accident – but no such thing. There was this middle-aged chap, protesting that there was no need for panic. He'd just felt tired and decided to have a nap. I asked where he was going and he said he was on his way to Upton-on-Severn for a point-to-point.

'That's tomorrow,' I said. 'I know – I'm walking it there from Monmouth.' The fellow intrigued me – so I offered him a lift to take a few miles off his journey. We had a brief chat and he told me he spent his life walking to point-to-point tracks. I had a few friends staying with me, and when I got home I was full of the story of 'my friend, the tramp'.

The following day, we all set off for the point-to-point at Upton, and just as we were driving over the bridge I noticed three policemen frog-marching a figure with bare feet, no trousers and a short mac. 'What's up,' I asked one of the policemen. 'He's just done a streak up the main street – he's bloody crackers.'

That was the last I saw of my hobo friend. I heard he was sent back to his 'home' in Monmouth.

Finally, to all my fellow jockeys, past and present, a word of advice – not from me but from pop singer Alvin Stardust. Alvin is a smashing guy who wrote an entertaining book called *Tales from the Saddle* in aid of the Save The Children Fund. When I met him, Alvin had been really bitten by the riding bug and had paid his dues with a few falls while under instruction. It all led to a nice piece of philosophy.

'Horse-riding,' said Alvin, 'is the perfect way of relaxing and taking your mind away from problems. You just sit there and let the horse do all the work, but you can't think of anything else or you fall off.'

Now you know, gentlemen.

CRICKET

K eeping wicket at Edgbaston on a Test Match ground has to be one of the highlights of my cricket career – but it almost finished me off. We went out to field, and as I was adjusting my gloves I half-heard the public address system say '. . . and opening the bowling from the pavilion end is Ward.' As this chap Ward was vanishing into the distance to reach the start of his run-up, Warwickshire and England batsman John Jameson, who was fielding at first slip, noticed that I was preparing to stand up to the wicket.

'What are you doing there, Terry?' enquired John politely but obviously surprised. 'I always stand up, John. I keep better that way,' said I confidently. 'If I were you, Terry, I'd move back a few yards. This fellow's a bit quick, you know.'

Reluctantly, I backed off and waited for the first ball. I doubt if the batsman saw it. I certainly didn't. I just felt a searing pain at the top of my right thigh as the new ball dug into my flesh. I hobbled around until the tea interval, and when I got back to the pavilion the more knowledgeable members of our team were saying it was a good job Ward was only bowling at half pace. As I inspected the ugly, red bruise half an inch from my groin, it dawned on me that I had been keeping wicket to Alan Ward of Derbyshire and England – reputed to be the quickest bowler in the country at the time. And I have to say it was the nearest I've ever been to becoming a gelding.

One of the Jockeys' XI regular matches was at Wislow Green – always a needle match. Come the last over we needed six to win and Biddlecombe and David Nicholson were in, batting 10 and 11. The bowler was at the end of his run-up, when Nicholson suddenly thrust his hand in the air and then walked off towards the pavilion. Captain for the day Josh Gifford was sitting in front of the pavilion, and as Nicholson approached he called out: 'Do we go for them or not, skipper?' 'Of course we do, you daft bugger,' came the reply. Nicholson trudged back to the square, called me for a conference and whispered: 'Tactical ploy – now let's get them.' He did – off the first two balls.

After one of our more notable cricketing triumphs, we decided to celebrate in the traditional fashion – drinks long into the night followed by a card school. The following morning, the poker school was still in session when we heard Macer Gifford coming downstairs after a few hours' sleep, coughing and spluttering as only a hung-over jockey can. For those of us who'd seen off the night, it was silly-bugger time. 'Pee in that champagne bottle, Terry,' said one of the card players, 'and we'll offer it to Macer.'

The deed done, Macer spotted the bottle and grunted: 'Christ, I could do with a drop of that.' He took a huge swig from the bottle, licked his lips and opined: 'It could do with being a little more chilled.' We never did let on to Macer why!

A match in the Cotswolds and Jeff King decided to leave his car parked at David Nicholson's house in Condicote. After the game and a good few drinks, Jeff and his passenger John Buckingham were given a lift back to David's to drive home. Now Condicote is somewhat remote, but Kingy was in no mood to take detailed instructions for his homeward route. It was into the car and away.

An hour later – and it was now past midnight – the sleeping Nicholsons were aroused by the sound of a car outside the house. Kingy had gone round in a circle. The knocks on the Nicholson front door were ignored and the place remained in darkness. Much cursing took place and David, peeking through the bedroom curtains, watched an irate Mr King reverse his car into the stone wall bordering the village green. Eventually the frustrated travellers decided to sleep in the car – and resumed their journey at first light at 5.30 a.m.

I was at Lords one day enjoying watching England against the West Indies in the company of Messrs Nicholson and Gifford. About halfway through the afternoon session came a loudspeaker announcement: 'Would Terry Biddlecombe, David Nicholson and Josh Gifford please report to the Secretary's office.' We got there to be told that we had been invited to the West Indies dressing room during the tea interval and would we join them at the Waldorf after play had ended for the day. Sir Garfield Sobers, the West Indies captain, was a keen horse-racing fan and we were given regal hospitality at the Waldorf.

Where I made my mistake was to switch the conversation with Sobers from horse-racing to cricket, and I offered the opinion rather loudly that I couldn't understand how Wes Hall was frightening the life out of England's batsmen. Suddenly I felt the slipstream of something hurtling just past my right ear and turned to see a cricket ball crash into the wall behind me. As I turned back, my face going paler by the second, I saw across the room a set of flashing white teeth in the middle of a beaming black face. 'That's how, Terry,' shouted Wes Hall.

Postscript

I've retired from regular cricket these days. The occasional appearance for the ex-Jockeys' XI is all I will consider. I knew my days were numbered a couple of years ago when I offered to keep wicket for the Central Television Sports Department in a charity six-a-side tournament at the Griff and Coton ground in Nuneaton.

In the dressing room before play, it was decided by a majority vote of five-to-one that a fourteen-stone Biddlecombe would not be as efficient behind the stumps as Mike Inman, a young pal of mine at Central who is an excellent soccer goalkeeper when he's not injured. So Mike kept wicket and I sulked in the field. But in six-a-side matches, every fielder has to bowl an over and I decided that if this was to be the end of a glorious career, I would give them all something to remember.

I needed only one ball to prove I should have been keeping wicket. It travelled yards over the head of the astonished batsman, was still gaining height as it passed over the wicket-keeper and went first bounce for four byes. For me it was good-bye.

TRAINERS

*F*alling off on the racecourse is bad enough, but getting buried while schooling at home can be more embarrassing – the stable jockey on the floor in full view of trainer, lads and work-riders. My worst moment came towards the end of my career when I was riding for Fulke Walwyn – a master trainer who regarded it as a cardinal sin if a horse fell while schooling.

Fulke decided he wanted me to school Amarind, a nice big chestnut horse who'd been in America, over fences. We had another novice upsides and a handicapper as the lead horse, and we all popped over three baby fences without any discomfort. Then we turned to take on the three big fences – as difficult as you'll find anywhere on a schooling ground. The other novice went at the first, the lead horse ran out at the second and Amarind was left on his own.

Knowing Fulke's reservations, I thought I'd pull up but I said to myself: 'Bugger it, he's jumped okay so far, let's kick on.' The inevitable happened. Amarind lunged at the fence, sank to his knees and I went straight over the handlebars. There's often a moment in that half-world as you pick yourself up dazed after a fall when you have a flash of inspiration. Fulke will go bloody barmy, I told myself. How can I get out of this? Then it came to me. I hid behind the fence. It must have looked like a scene from a farce as I crouched there, giggling, but it had the desired effect. Fulke came across, growled something I couldn't understand and trooped off to breakfast.

Jockeys never like their telephone numbers to be too well known. There's always the danger of calls from cranks and disgruntled punters – and the nuisance of people calling just when you are tucked up in bed for an early night. I've given a few evening callers a flea in their ear, but I have to own up to one of my biggest *faux-pas* when the former Royal trainer Peter Cazalet rang me. In my defence, it must be said that I'd been pestered by a few waste-of-time calls and I'd just gone through a bad day with a fall which I feared might put me out of the Grand National meeting at Liverpool.

I'd just turned in for the night when the phone rang and the voice at the other end said: 'Peter Cazalet, here. I want you to ride a horse for me in the Mildmay at Aintree.' I'd never ridden for Peter Cazalet, nor had he ever asked me. So I decided it was someone winding me up – and told the caller, impolitely, to go away. The thought did cross my mind that the call might have been genuine – but I dismissed it because I was just another young jockey at the time and I'd never dreamt of riding a Cazalet horse.

I discovered the error of my ways soon after arriving in the weighing-room at Aintree on Mildmay day. It was common knowledge that Biddlecombe had discourteously turned down Peter Cazalet. Stan Mellor was offered the ride, accepted and won on it. Not surprisingly Peter Cazalet never rang me again – and I never rode one of his horses.

Willie Stephenson was a great trainer on the flat and over the sticks. He won the Derby with Arctic Prince, the Grand National with Oxo and the Champion Hurdle three times with Sir Ken. But my favourite tale about 'Uncle Willie' concerns one of his legendary betting coups at humble Market Rasen.

David Nicholson – up and coming at the time – rode one of Willie's hurdlers called Granville at Kempton on Boxing Day and finished unplaced. Three weeks later Willie rang David and said: 'Michael Scudamore will pick you up at half past six tomorrow morning. You're riding for me at Market Rasen.' Michael and David arrived early and Willie ordered them both to walk the course. Then he told Michael he would ride Cool Debate, which duly won, and David would have the mount on Granville.

Before the race, a horse called Silver Sand, trained by Fred Armstrong, was reckoned to be a certainty – and just to make sure Fred jocked off the young Josh Gifford and gave the ride to hurdles expert Johnny Gilbert. But it was Granville who won the race after being backed from 33-1 to 7-2. To this day, David Nicholson's eyes sparkle when he talks about the mountain of notes he saw being displayed by Granville's connections on a tressle table in the tea bar after racing. And I'm told that Fred Armstrong was so crestfallen by the outcome, he stalked off to his car, drove away – and left Josh Gifford stranded at the track.

During my time as stable jockey with the great Fred Rimell at Kinnersley, we had a useful horse called Glenn. At work one morning, the gaffer kept on at me to keep the horse's head straight. Hard as I tried there was nothing I could do about it. Eventually Fred blew his top so I suggested, none too politely, that if he could do any better he should get up himself.

I never saw Fred ride a horse at work, but up he got. They cantered two furlongs up, two furlongs back– with Glenn's head going everywhere but straight. After fighting his losing battle, Fred handed the horse back to me with the words: 'He must have been born like it.' Trainers, as most jockeys will tell you until they become trainers, are never wrong!

A trainer better known for his exploits in National Hunt racing could perhaps be forgiven for perpetrating the *faux-pas* of the 1985 flat season. In March he told the owner of a promising three-year-old colt: 'I want to give him a couple of runs to get him right for the Wood Ditton.' It was left to the owner to point out that the Wood Ditton Stakes, run at Newmarket every April, is for unraced three-year-olds.

Slightly embarrassing – but not as costly as the case of mistaken identity which afflicted a leading Irish trainer, who had been working some of his horses after racing at Naas. He mistook an interested onlooker, who had replaced a couple of divots, for the groundsman, gave him £20 and said: 'Very good ground, Paddy – you're doing a wonderful job.'

Then there was the National Hunt trainer, after being told I'd declared a breast-plate on his horse on the advice of the head lad, asking me: 'Where do I put it?' 'Slip it over his tail, sir,' I told him.

In 1980 Prince Charles rode Nick Gaselee's horse Sea Swell into fourth place in a chase at Sandown, and the Lambourn trainer now has an amusing reminder of the occasion in pride of place on his dining-room wall.

It is the original version of the 'JAK' cartoon which appeared in the *Daily Express* the morning after the race. It shows Prince Charles having breakfast with the Queen and the Duke of Edinburgh with the caption: 'And the Queen Mum's not pleased either. She had fifty pence on the nose.' The framed cartoon was sent to Nick by his friend Simon Parker-Bowles, who added his own caption: 'Must do better next time, Nick!'

An owner who had horses with a leading Epsom trainer unexpectedly returned home on leave from military service shortly after the Second World War. It was Derby week and he rang the trainer to ask if he could use his influence to provide a badge for Epsom on Derby Day. 'No problem,' said the trainer.

A polite request was made to the Clerk of the Course, stressing that the owner was having a few days away from the rigours of the Army. It was promptly turned down. Said the aggrieved trainer to the Clerk of the Course:

'Sir, there's only one difference between you and a bucket of shit and that's the bucket.' Having got that off his chest, the trainer was reported to the stewards and fined a fiver. I'm sure it was worth every penny.

Jenny Pitman has done for lady trainers what Chrissy Evert did for women tennis players. She has put them in the big league. Jenny and I go back a long way and her marvellous success with horses like Corbiere and Burrough Hill Lad has come as no surprise to me. Jenny is not only a highly accomplished trainer, she is also a first-class judge of horses and form. She upsets a few people because she says exactly what she thinks – and I found this out very early in our relationship.

In her younger days Jenny worked for Major Champneys' stable and she used to lead up a useful horse called Riversdale, a smashing performer owned by the late Dick Brazil. Jenny was always very jolly, but if she thought you hadn't given Riversdale a very good ride she would say so in no uncertain manner. I suppose I was the first of many jockeys to feel the sharp edge of Jenny Pitman's tongue.

Jenny led up Riversdale when I won on him at Sandown and Kempton, and some time later I was at a jockey's dance at Newbury when I saw her in the company of Richard Pitman. They came over and Pip said: 'Terry, I'd like you to meet my fiancée. Jenny, this is Terry Biddlecombe.' 'No need for introductions,' said Jenny, 'I know this bugger. He still owes me two quid for leading up winners for him.'

Mind you, I've repaid Jenny since then. When Corbiere was being prepared for the 1985 Grand National, Jenny decided to try and sweeten him up by giving him a regular outing with the local hunt in Berkshire. Jenny invited me to ride Corbiere in the hunting field as a feature for my horse-racing spot on Central Television Sport. Corbiere is such a noble animal that it was a privilege for me – but, as I told Jenny afterwards, even his Grand National weight – which she so loudly criticized – must have come as relief after having the Biddlecombe of 1985 on his back.

Just over a year earlier, I was at Jenny's Weathercock House stables in Lambourn to film a feature on Burrough Hill Lad during the week leading up to the Cheltenham Gold Cup. Jenny had told me five months earlier when we were watching him work after racing at Wolverhampton that she thought Burrough Hill Lad could be a Gold Cup horse, and after his impressive wins in races like the Welsh Grand National he was favourite for the Cheltenham prize. But as Cheltenham approached there were persistent rumours that Burrough Hill Lad was breaking blood vessels. I spoke to Jenny and she said: 'Get your cameras down here and watch him work and I'll soon show you whether he's bursting.'

When I arrived at Weathercock House at seven a.m. Jenny was in a foul mood. There were more rumours of her horse breaking blood vessels and the morning newspapers were being thrown around the kitchen. There was only a week to go before the Gold Cup, but Jenny put Burrough Hill Lad through strong work on the Downs and then Phil Tuck popped him over six of the big schooling fences.

As Burrough Hill Lad finished his morning's work, Jenny called over the cameraman and said: 'Stick that camera up his nose and you can prove to the whole bloody world that he's not breaking blood vessels.' Jenny did an interview and told Central's viewers: 'I'm more confident about Burrough Hill Lad winning the Gold Cup than I ever was about Corbiere winning last year's Grand National.' I wasn't about to argue with her and although I'd fancied Wayward Lad for ages, Jenny persuaded me to change my mind. She was right – of course.

Jenny Pitman trained a useful chaser called Esban, who was owned by the singer Dorothy Squires. Miss Squires always insisted to Jenny that her horse made the running and Jenny carried out her instructions – until one day at Warwick. Esban was running in the Crudwell Cup over three miles and five furlongs and Jenny instructed jockey Ally Branford: 'Whatever the owner says to you today, just ignore it. I don't want to make the running. Settle the horse third or fourth and ride a normal race on him.'

As the field was going down the far side for the first time, Johnny Suthern, who had previously ridden Esban, came upsides Ally and said: 'Who's going to get a bollocking, then?' But Ally stuck to the trainer's instructions and Esban won the race easily – much to the delight of his owner.

Jenny's instructions had a rather different result at Doncaster one day, when she had two horses in a two and three quarter-mile hurdle – Bossal, ridden by Brian Smart, and Spartacus, ridden by her sister Mandy. Before the race Jenny told Mandy: 'Wherever Smarty goes, you go with him.' What neither of them bargained for was that Bossal was about to take off with Smarty, and Mandy, doing as she was told, did everything she could to stay with them. The situation was made worse by Smarty trying to tell Mandy that he couldn't hold his horse and Mandy trying to get closer because she couldn't hear what he was saying. With Jenny in hysterics in the stands, Bossal finally burned off Spartacus and everything else with Smarty still trying to hold him as they flew past the winning post well clear.

The strange case of the Lambourn 'cock-napping' began under the cover of darkness. A raiding party from the village advanced on Jenny Pitman's stables and by first light, the stone cockerel perched on the wall at the entrance to Weathercock House had disappeared. Mrs Pitman was not amused. Previous acts of vandalism had been tolerated without recourse to the law, but this was the last straw. The local constabulary was called in.

'What we have here, madam, is a case of wilful damage and technical theft,' was their summary. For days, fingers were pointed at likely suspects all around Lambourn, but it was only when Jenny took the law in her own hands that the culprits owned up. She let it be known that charges would be dropped if the offenders presented themselves at Weathercock House at six o'clock on Sunday evening, when she would sit in judgment.

First through the door was Tim Thompson Jones. 'I'm not surprised at you,' said Jenny. Next came Simon Sherwood. 'I am surprised at you.' And finally Jimmy Duggan. 'Who the bloody hell are you?' The three jockeys were given both barrels verbally. Then Jenny announced the punishment. She would drop all charges if each of them donated £100 to Riding for the Disabled and paid £75 costs to replace the cockerel. The cheques written, that was that – except for a parting shot from Mrs P.

'By the way,' she told the chastised trio as they left, 'I chose Riding for the Disabled because if I catch you round here again, you'll be needing them.'

Mercy Rimell is another lady trainer whom I admire and respect greatly. I have, of course, known Mercy for many years both professionally and socially. She is a charming lady and fascinating company at the dinner table – but she can be absolutely withering if you invoke her displeasure.

During the autumn of 1984, I took a film crew to Mercy's stables at Kinnersley in Worcestershire to watch her 1983 Champion Hurdle winner Gaye Brief beginning his comeback from injury. The three-man crew was in position near the finish of the all-weather gallop when the rain started pouring down. Instinctively, the electrician with the crew reacted by putting up a huge, coloured golf umbrella. I sensed the problem immediately. You can put up an umbrella as Nick Faldo is about to sink a crucial putt at Wentworth or as Nicki Lauda is roaring past you at 160 m.p.h. at Silverstone, but on Mercy Rimell's gallops as you are being approached by one of the most valuable hurdlers in the world, you are better advised to get wet.

Before I could utter a word of warning to the innocent, Mercy came over the rise on Comedy of Errors, another former Champion Hurdler she now rides as her hack. She looked one way and saw Gaye Brief galloping towards us – and the other way at the umbrella, which somehow seemed to be getting bigger and more conspicuous by the second. She dealt with the problem succinctly. 'YOU. . . .' she bellowed. 'Get that bloody umbrella down. Where do you think you are – Blackpool beach?'

Ron Peachey, head lad at Fred Rimell's during most of my time at Kinnersley, had been giving me some stick one day, so I decided to repay him when I went to his house for dinner. I'd promised Ron a bottle of my best port and that's exactly what he got – the bottle. I had just finished a beautiful bottle of 1948 vintage, so I filled it with some rough old port off the wood, laced it with brandy and re-corked it.

After dinner I left Ron to enjoy his 'vintage' port at his leisure. I feared the worst the following morning, but Ron came across to me full of smiles. 'That port was beautiful, Terry,' he said. 'I can tell it was good because it hasn't given me a headache.' I never did tell him it was from Chateau Biddlecombe.

Peter Walwyn, the popular Lambourn trainer, won the 1976 Champion Stakes at Newmarket with a horse called Vitiges for the French owner *M.* Marc Laloum. The victory called for a celebration and *M.* Laloum hosted a memorable evening at The Bell at Sutton Benger in Wiltshire. Being a polite sort, Peter was calling his owner '*Monsieur* Laloum' when he was invited to be less formal. '*Je m'appelle Marc*,' he said. 'Big Pete', as the guvnor of Seven Barrows is universally known, responded in kind.

'*Je me'appelle Grand Pete*.' 'I think not,' said *M.* Laloum. 'In French that translates as Big Fart.'

I am indebted to Peter Walwyn for recently revealing a more poetic side to his character by offering me this 'Ode to an Amateur Rider' (which I am assured is not dedicated to his assistant trainer Tim Thompson Jones):

-

> His legs were long,
> His seat was loose,
> His knees were knocking
> from self-abuse.
> But he rode through his field
> Like shit from a goose
> And won the length of his doo-da.

-

On the subject of 'seats' and amateur riders, I'm reminded of the story of Lord John Oaksey's first day riding work for Fulke Walwyn. Back at the breakfast table, John asked Fulke: 'Did I do alright?' Said Fulke: 'You have a good old-fashioned seat – a bit like the one on my lavatory.'

Peter Walwyn must have thought a new, wealthy owner had landed on his doorstep, when a huge, chauffeur-driven, left-hand-drive Mercedes pulled onto his drive at Seven Barrows and out stepped a gentleman in flowing Arab robes, accompanied by a stunning blonde. Their appearance in Lambourn had made such an impact, I'm told that there had been bows and curtseys when they stopped for petrol in the village. Certainly Peter was impressed – until his 'new owners' let him off the hook and revealed all. The visitors were, in fact, two of Peter's regular guests – trainer Mark Smyly from nearby Kingswood House and Fiona Vigors, wife of Upper Lambourn trainer, Nick.

Peter was so impressed that he attempted to try a similar ruse on David Nicholson during a Sunday visit to the Cotswolds. Unfortunately he chose the wrong day to pose as an Arab caller at Condicote. The place was packed with visitors for David's annual open day and after seeing through Peter's disguise very quickly, a disenchanted 'Duke' promptly ordered him to bugger off.

When See You Then broke the course record to win the 1985 Champion Hurdle at Cheltenham, trainer Nicky Henderson won £38,030 in prize money – and a Silk Cut King Size from me. A fortnight earlier I'd been at Brean Sands in Somerset watching Nicky's string work along the beach. With local trainer, the genial Bert House, providing expert advice on the tides, Brean Sands was one of the few places you could exercise horses during that dreadful February freeze.

The morning I was there they could have staged a Champion Hurdle trial along the beach. Mercy Rimell took Gaye Brief there, Jim Old was working Cima and Sally Oliver was putting Amarach through his paces. But it was See You Then who took my eye – and Nicky Henderson who took my cigarettes. He'd set off so early from Lambourn to reach the seaside by 7.30 that he'd forgotten his cigarettes and spent all morning smoking mine – a strange reversal of roles, I'll admit.

Back in Bert House's lounge, where a scotch or two was getting the morning chill out of our systems, Nicky asked whether I shared the general opinion that Monica Dickinson's Browne's Gazette was a good thing for the Champion Hurdle. I said that I thought Browne's Gazette would be beaten at Cheltenham. 'Well if Browne's Gazette doesn't win it, mine will,' said Nicky. Since I strongly fancied Gaye Brief at the time, I replied: 'If See You Then wins, I'll give you another cigarette.' I paid up at four o'clock at Cheltenham on Champion Hurdle day.

I try never to smoke before midday. In fact some people reckon I try never to smoke my own cigarettes at any time of the day. Michael Oliver, who trains some useful horses at Hartlebury in Worcestershire, reminded me of my reputation recently. It was a few days before the Grand National and I was at Michael's yard to ride out the Aintree favourite West Tip for my television spot. I'd ridden the horse two-and-a-half years earlier just after he'd won first time out in a novice hurdle at Warwick – a 50-1 success which came only three months after he'd almost been killed in a collision with an articulated lorry while road-walking. I was impressed by how powerfully West Tip had developed during those two-and-a-half years, and the old nerve began to twitch a little when I realized the responsibility of riding him with the Grand National so near.

'Do you think I can have one of your cigarettes before you give me a leg up, Michael?' I asked. 'The last time you asked me for a cigarette was sixteen years ago when I worked at Fred Rimell's – and I see you're still begging them,' said Michael. 'Yes, I can vaguely remember you at Kinnersley, Michael. You only stayed about a month.' 'That's right – I couldn't afford to keep you in cigarettes,' replied Michael as he gave me a leg up on West Tip.

Johnny Buckingham, who won that memorable 1967 Grand National on the 100-1 shot Foinavon, would readily endorse Michael Oliver's view. While Johnny was a jockey, and afterwards when he became a valet, he was always my favourite target in the weighing-room as provider of the Biddlecombe fags. The day I retired, Johnny came up to me, shook my hand, offered me a cigarette and said: 'That's 870 you owe me now.'

Other people's fags are one thing, other people's colours quite another. Epsom trainer 'Nat' Smyth – whose son Ron has carried on a winning family tradition under both codes – was called on by a potential owner, enquiring about buying his first horse. Nat went through all the formalities, the new owner signed an authority to act and commissioned the trainer to purchase a horse on his behalf. A couple of drinks later, everything was settled and the new owner was just about to leave when he asked: 'What about colours?' 'Come over here,' said Nat and opened a cupboard full of racing silks in various colours. 'Take your pick from these,' he invited. 'But don't they all belong to someone?' asked the new owner. 'Sure they do,' said Nat, 'but they're all either dead or skint.'

Arthur Goodwill was always an entertaining character during his many years as a trainer at Newmarket. He trained on the flat and always kept a few on the go for the National Hunt season. I rode a couple of winners for Arthur, who, for reasons we won't go into, is universally known as 'Fiddler', and we had some great times together.

It seems that, in retirement, Fiddler has lost neither his liking for a tilt at the bookmakers nor his sense of humour. Two days into a Guineas meeting at Newmarket, Fiddler was asked how his encounters with the ring were going. 'I had a good day yesterday, not so good today. But I reckon if you can get out of bed in the morning, you're winning every day.'

Ian Balding, whose superb training establishment at Kingsclere in Berkshire houses some of the best horses in the country including many of the Queen's thoroughbreds, has always fancied his chances as a jockey. Ian is a regular rider in hunter chases and points, but he'll probably want to forget the day he rode to hounds with me across Castlemorton Common beneath the Malverns.

He had sent a couple of horses to me and one of them was a point-to-pointer, whom we called Spots. He was a big, strong horse and a ferocious puller. Ian was on his back as we set off at Castlemorton, and before very long Spots took off. As they passed me Ian proudly shouted: 'There goes that man Balding again.' From my vantage point, I knew they were heading for trouble. Spots was totally out of control and they were approaching unknown territory. Before I could warn him, Ian came across one of Castlemorton's notorious hidden ditches. Spots stumbled and Ian did about ten somersaults before hitting the deck. As I cantered past, I saw the sorry sight of a Royal trainer limping home.

Martin and Edna Tate, good friends of mine, run a successful training establishment at Chaddesley Corbett in Worcestershire. Before they started winning top races with good horses like the chaser Scot Lane and the hurdler Bajan Sunshine, their career began as permit-holders, pursuing the more modest prizes around the smaller tracks. And as most permit-holders – myself included – know, the bigger trainers never relish being beaten by them.

After winning their first two races, the Tates were confronted in the unsaddling enclosure by a well-known Midlands trainer, smiling through clenched teeth. On both occasions, the congratulations came with a sting in the tail: 'Well done – bloody bad race, though!'

Next time, Edna Tate knew how to deal with her patronising adversary. After winner number three, the trainer only got as far as 'Well done . . .'. Immediately Edna chipped in: 'Yes, but it was a bloody bad race, wasn't it?' The Tates have won a lot of bloody bad races since that day – and a lot of bloody good races as well.

Some of the old-timers in National Hunt racing never cease to be amazed at the way we pamper horses these days. What with weighing them every day, giving them physiotherapy from a portable machine once a week, replacing the traditional shavings by lining their boxes with shredded newspapers or toilet rolls, most of them live a five-star existence. Even the menus are changing. We shove protein into them and the old diet of oats, hay and mash is being replaced by racehorse cubes – with everything they need in a bowl of little brown nuggets, no doubt all worked out by computer.

A trainer singing the praises of racehorse cubes to me claimed they had transformed one of his handicappers into a star – and I was impressed when it won four on the trot. Mind you that was before the handicapper caught up with the racehorse cubes and the horse then went twelve months without getting in the frame.

I'll leave the last word to a friend of mine, who, for many years, has been a highly successful permit-holder from a yard even an estate agent wouldn't describe as having every mod. con. 'There's only one way horses should eat – and that's off the floor. I chuck the oats on the floor, the hay on the floor and leave them a bucket of water. What they don't eat, the rats can have.'

Put that into your computer.

HORSES

Despite all the great horses I rode, two of the more moderate performers stand out strongly in my memory. Dundalk, once with Fred Rimell and then trained by Doug Francis in Cheshire, and Honey End, trained by Earl Jones at Hednesford in Staffordshire, both brought up a century of winners for me in successive seasons. It was a great honour for me because I was the first National Hunt jockey to ride 100 winners in consecutive seasons, but both rides had their funny side.

I rode Dundalk in the Bettisfield Handicap Chase at Bangor on 24 April 1965, and I had been stuck on ninety-nine winners for four days. Doug Francis offered me the ride on Dundalk, I knew the horse well from his time at Kinnersley and everyone was reasonably confident of success.

Dundalk duly won and I had become only the fourth jockey in National Hunt history to ride 100 winners in a season – joining the élite company of Fred Rees, Fred Winter and Stan Mellor. The crowd at Bangor realized this and when I rode into the winner's enclosure there was a tumultuous reception. Dundalk's owner, a Cheshire farmer, turned to Doug Francis and said that all the cheering had amazed him. 'I never realized I had so many friends,' he said. Doug, never a man to mince words, replied: 'It's nothing to do with you, you silly bugger – that's Biddlecombe's hundredth winner.'

Just over a year later, I was desperate to reach my century again and time was running out. It was the second week in June and the season was almost over. I'd travelled over 80,000 miles, taking rides here, there and everywhere, and I was beginning to feel that I'd just miss out. I rang a lot of trainers for rides, and when I noticed that the chaser Honey End was engaged at Uttoxeter on 11 June, I asked Earl Jones if I could ride him. Earl won't mind my saying that he's a bit of an acquired taste. He's a fiery Irishman who says what he thinks – and little did I know that he'd been waiting for Biddlecombe.

'It's the first time you've spoken to me for three years since you became big-time, so you can bugger off. I've got a jockey for Honey End,' said Earl. I retreated with a flea in my ear, but Earl's jockey Jimmy Fitzgerald told me that he didn't mind standing down and he'd have a word with the trainer. By the time I got to Uttoxeter, Earl had been persuaded to agree to compromise.

51

'Tell Biddlecombe to get down on his knees and ask me for the ride. Otherwise I'll sack you and neither of you will ride it,' Earl told Fitz. I was suitably chastised, met Earl's conditions without quite going on bended knee and we have been great friends ever since.

Honey End won the Midsummer Chase to bring up my second century, but I only had time for one small glass of champagne before I dashed off to ride at an evening meeting at Market Rasen. My pals in the weighing-room were going on about the lack of celebrations for Biddlecombe's new record, so I offered to take Michael Scudamore, Josh Gifford and Roy Blandford into Lincoln for a meal and good few drinks. I don't know whether the sedate city of Lincoln has changed much, but in June 1966 it wasn't the place to go for a celebration, racing-style. The only place we could find open was a Chinese restaurant without a drinks licence. So we celebrated the most memorable landmark in my career with chow mein and Coca Cola.

Even the best judges in racing are wrong sometimes and I'm glad to say that my father, Walter, got it wrong on the day that mattered most to me. It was the 1967 Gold Cup at Cheltenham. I was on Woodland Venture, owned by Harry Collins and trained by Fred Rimell, in a small but class field which included Mill House and Stalbridge Colonist. I knew Woodland Venture well. He was a great galloper and a good jumper – but occasionally he would take it into his head to demolish a fence or two.

Gold Cup day was the first time Dad had been racing for years, and he was standing with a friend by the first fence. When we got there, Woodland Venture never rose a leg. He went straight through the fence and even smashed the guard rail in half. Dad turned to his friend and said: 'If the lad has got to ride that round, he's got no chance.' His opinion wouldn't have changed when we smashed straight through the second, but then Woodland Venture settled down. We went round upsides David Nicholson on Mill House chatting about the prospect of being on the Cheltenham Christmas cards – but Christmas never came for Duke. Mill House departed at the last ditch and left me in front.

It was much too soon for Woodland Venture to be out on his own, but swinging into the straight there was only one thing to do – kick like hell. Once I was in the straight at Cheltenham I never waited for anyone. I sensed a challenger would appear – and, sure enough, by the time we were approaching the last Stan Mellor and the grey Stalbridge Colonist loomed upsides. We

52

jumped the last together and Stan headed me for a few strides, but Woodland Venture quickened to the front again and we just held them.

Dad was the first man in the paddock. 'That must have been some ride,' he said. Praise indeed – particularly when you've been written off at the first.

Fred Rimell also trained a horse called Gypsy Lad – and the first time we realized there was something wrong with him was the morning he nearly killed me. I was schooling him at Kinnersley and he absolutely buried me. I eventually struggled to my feet and found that although I could walk, I couldn't see – and perhaps that was a clue. By the time I'd come round to my senses and had a cup of coffee, we realized that Gypsy Lad had gone blind in one eye.

My problems with the horse didn't end there – he was the cause of what Fred Rimell reckoned was the worst race I ever rode. It was at Uttoxeter, and because of Gypsy Lad's disability I felt he needed a bit of light and a bit of room so I went round the outside on him. I suppose I gave him too much to do, but I thought it was the best way to ride the horse. Anyway we got beaten when Fred thought we should have won. He told me so in no uncertain fashion. 'That should have won – but you've been all over England,' was Fred's summary of the race.

It didn't end there. When I got home from Uttoxeter at about 5.30, Mercy Rimell telephoned me. 'Terry, you must get over here immediately – Fred is doing his nut.' So I drove over and we had a long chat. Fred said his piece, I said mine. Then, like the gentleman he was, he started pouring the drinks, we both got merry, shook hands and I went home.

Charlie Potheen was a horse who frightened the life out of me. Trained by Fulke Walwyn he was a big awkward horse, and there were times when you just couldn't do anything with him. He hung worse than anything I ever rode, then he would cock his jaw coming to a fence, and if you stayed on you were lucky. I won good races on him and finished third behind The Dikler and Pendil in the 1973 Gold Cup, but it was always a hair-raising experience.

To say that Charlie Potheen liked to make the running is putting it mildly – he would take off like a bat out of hell. At Doncaster in January 1973 I rode Charlie in the Great Yorkshire Chase. We took off, as usual, at 100 m.p.h. and Tommy Stack on Clever Scot, another confirmed front-runner, came with us. As we hurtled towards the first fence, I shouted to Tommy: 'If we get over the first three, we'll finish up in the middle of Doncaster.' Charlie and I burned off Clever Scot and then he stayed on gallantly to beat Spanish Steps.

Others had mastered Charlie Potheen occasionally. Richard Pitman had won the Hennessey Gold Cup at Newbury on him before I ever sat on the horse. Others had inevitably had problems with him – I remember Charlie

taking Stan Mellor through the rails at Cheltenham. But I doubt if anyone ever came closer to the weighing-room in the sky riding Charlie Potheen than I did in the Hermitage Chase at Newbury in October 1973.

He cocked his jaw going towards the last ditch and when I pulled him round he galloped straight into the ditch. Straight away the lights went out and many people at Newbury that day, as I learned later, reckoned they'd never seen a worse fall. Charlie Potheen was never the same horse again after damaging his neck and back. I felt like I'd damaged everything, but apart from the bumps and bruises, it turned out to be nothing worse than four fractured ribs.

Six months later I retired – and the ditch at Newbury had a lot to do with my decision.

I had more feeling for Coral Diver than any other horse I ever rode. He was as tough and game as they come, a bit of a character, and we always understood each other – probably because we were so alike. I could talk to Coral Diver during a race and he would listen – most of the time. When he got a little too sure of himself, I would growl at him: 'Eh, don't take the piss,' and he would settle down again.

Coral Diver ran on the flat for Pat Rohan and then his owner Bryan Jenks sent him to Fred Rimell. I won on him first time out over hurdles at Doncaster, and we went on to win the Victor Ludorum at Haydock, the National Spirit Hurdle at Fontwell and the Christmas Hurdle at Kempton. But the race that typified Coral Diver and our relationship was the 1969 *Daily Express* Triumph Hurdle at Cheltenham. From a mile out I'd been hard at work on him physically and niggling at him verbally, and I doubted whether we would last out up the hill. Then he flew the last and I swear the bugger looked round and winked at me before taking hold of his bridle, pricking his ears and producing a winning sprint.

Bryan Jenks gave Coral Diver to me when he retired from National Hunt as an eight-year-old. And he became even more of a character in his old age. On his good days, he was the ideal lead horse for my young breakers; on his bad days, I took him back to his box because I didn't want him teaching the young horses his tricks. One day a lady owner called to see me and was fascinated by the presence of Coral Diver in my yard. She walked over to his box and gave him a polo mint – and he promptly thrust his head forward and took a bite at her ample bosom. She dined out on the story for months: 'There I was at Biddlecombe's, I give Coral Diver a polo mint and he bites my right tit. No, not Biddlecombe – the horse.'

Coral Diver was still sound enough to run in point-to-points, so I decided I'd try to go for a touch with him. He first ran at Ledbury when he wasn't quite ready, but if he hadn't made a mistake at the third last he would have won by a hundred yards. Next time, I said to myself, we'll go to Berkeley and he won't be beaten.

At this point, I should say that as a youngster my punting career had been brief and expensive. At Wincanton I'd shovelled a carefully saved £20 on a horse called Mumbo Jumbo, trained and ridden by my father and regarded by all the family as a good thing. Dad had the race won over the last, but he dropped his hands with a shade too much confidence on the run-in and was beaten in the last stride.

It had a drastic effect on my betting activities. An immediate halt was called after a lesson learned. But all those years later, Coral Diver at Berkeley wasn't just a good bet – he represented an investment. I risked £35 on it. Just as I started to count my winnings, my jockey went to sleep, left the old horse too much to do and punter Biddlecombe was back on the wagon.

I'd had Coral Diver for four years when I decided, in 1980, that my old pal wasn't sound enough to enjoy life any more. I asked my Dad to have him for a few weeks because I couldn't bear to see him leave for the knacker's yard. Four months later, I received a cheque for £450 in the post. I stood there and cried like a baby.

Normandy was another of my favourite horses – on the racecourse. At home he was a horrible little sod, but put him in a race and he was a real man. I was the first jockey to sit on him – and that was in the paddock before his first race at Kempton in February 1969. He won that and we formed a great partnership – highlighted by winning the Irish Sweeps Hurdle in January 1970. But much as I admired Normandy on the racecourse, he did have a split personality. At home he would cow-kick and bite anyone who went near him. They reckoned he nearly killed a lad in Ireland, and it was a brave man who ventured into Normandy's box.

After his racing career, Normandy was sold to Roy Edwards to go to stud. As the horse left Kinnersley, Fred Rimell warned Roy: 'Watch out for him or he'll have you.' It didn't take long for the warning to prove well-founded. Normandy had Roy cornered in his box – and my old riding pal had to sit there for three hours until rescuers appeared.

After Willie Carson had completed his recovery from a horrific fall on Silken Knot in the Yorkshire Oaks in August 1981, he had his first ride for me. His mount was The Pilgarlic, that old warrior of Aintree, across four furlongs of the common at Corse Lawn near my home. Willie had not been on a racehorse for more than four months, but 'Phyllis' – as we call our faithful old gelding at home – is a safe conveyance.

Before The Pilgarlic's owner Mrs Scotty Poole gave him to me, he'd finished third, fourth and fifth in the Grand National and I trained him to finish fourth in the Foxhunters. Few horses have jumped more fences around Aintree and while most people reckoned 'Phyllis' was too clever to fall, I reckoned he was too mean.

The only problem I envisaged with Willie riding him was that The Pilgarlic was not used to having such a lightweight jockey on his back. And as we hacked to the common, my wife Ann told Willie's wife Elaine: 'I hope Phyllis doesn't run away with Willie – he's a very strong old horse.' Her concern was not misplaced. After a furlong cantering 'Phyllis' decided to take off and my hunter decided to take him on. I was about half-a-length up and Willie yelled: 'What are you doing, Bidders. Hang on a bit.'

Suddenly we were approaching the road. 'What do we do now?' Willie shouted. 'You won't pull the bugger up – you'll have to jump it,' I replied. And that's just what they did. A breathless Willie Carson eventually pulled him up, the smile returned to his face and in less than a minute, he'd proved his nerve was as strong as ever. W. Carson was ready to take his supreme talent back to the flat.

The Pilgarlic's more regular partner has been Mrs A. Biddlecombe. She wanted to ride in point-to-points, so 'Phyllis' – with a little help from me – became her tutor. Ann had never ridden over fences at speed, so we taught her gently, schooled her over Mercy Rimell's jumps at Kinnersley and eventually she was ready for her competitive debut. We chose Garnon's point-to-point near Hereford. The Pilgarlic looked a picture, but on the way to the start Ann was trembling and I don't think I've ever been more nervous myself.

I accompanied them to the start because I wanted to make sure they jumped off. I gave 'Phyllis' a clout round the backside with my binocular case and they were on their way. To my immense relief they got round safely. Ann sat there, looking petrified, and 'Phyllis' did everything right. They finished within sight of the winner, Ann said she'd enjoyed it and I thought next time they'd be worth a bet.

We chose the Farmer's race at Ledbury and did everything we could in the way of preparation. The evening before the race, we drove around the course and only one fence worried me. I told Ann to take care at the ditch four from

home and if she got over that safely she'd win.

I have to admit that I went for a little touch and everything was fine – until they reached the ditch, four out. 'Phyllis' tried to paddle through it and, through my binoculars, I saw the unwelcome sight of my wife's posterior flying through the air. In the ensuing chaos, 'Phyllis' brought down the mount of Phillipa Bainbridge, daughter of the Joint Master, and then decided to make his own way home. He jumped over hedges and wire fences and by the time I got to his horsebox, he was standing there waiting for me – without a scratch.

Meanwhile, back at the ditch, my wife was crawling around on hands and knees in the company of two ambulance men. When I reached the scene, worried that she might be unable to stand, she calmly informed me: 'I've lost a contact lens.' I persuaded her to give up the search, and back in the weighing-room she reported she'd fallen. 'Rubbish,' I said, 'you were unseated.' It was a harsh judgment and probably hid my relief that horse and jockey, while a little sore in some embarrassing places, were still in one piece. I reckon that was the end of Ann's point-to-point career. She says she's willing to give it another try – providing she can have lessons from John Francome.

I've seen novice horses end up in some strange places around the racecourse after losing their pilot – but only one went for a swim. Josh Gifford trained a four-year-old filly called Sea Pearl, a nice sort I had bred from Pearldom, a mare who cost me only £200. So as I stood next to Josh watching Sea Pearl run in a novice hurdle at Worcester, I had more than a passing interest in her progress.

We were both disappointed when Sea Pearl dropped her jockey at the far end of the course, but there was worse to come. She took off, ran out of the course and dived straight into the River Severn. Josh, Sea Pearl's lad and myself sprinted 200 yards round the back of the stands and saw Sea Pearl being taken up the river by the high tide.

She was fighting like hell to get to the bank, but she was still carrying her saddle with twelve stone in the weight-cloth. We tried wading in to get to her, and the lad even swam into the middle of the river. By now a large crowd had gathered on the bank and finally Sea Pearl somehow managed to reach safety. We caught hold of her and helped her scramble up the bank – a rescue accompanied by the kind of cheering normally associated with a well-backed winner going past the post.

The only physical damage on the filly was a cut leg, although everyone feared that the mental scars would ruin her racing career. But Sea Pearl, from the Biddlecombe breed, was made of sterner stuff. Josh got her fit again and eighteen months later she came back to Worcester, decided against going for a swim — and won a novices chase.

Horses often make a habit of proving you wrong and sometimes they can even divide opinion within a stable. Bossal, a hurdler who joined Jenny Pitman's yard after winning a couple of races on the flat, was just that kind of controversial character.

First time out over hurdles, he bolted in at Doncaster, but every time he worked he would duck and dive at the hurdles, and one day on Lambourn's schooling ground a radio broadcast crew, doing a profile on Jenny, watched in amazement when Bossal unshipped his rider and dragged him halfway round Berkshire. Jenny was sure that the horse needed blinkers, but Brian Smart, who was stable jockey at the time, insisted that Bossal should not be branded as a rogue.

Smarty made the point very forcibly after Bossal had fallen at the last when looking certain to win another race at Doncaster. He came back to the paddock and said: 'Don't let me hear anyone calling this horse a shit. If anyone ever questions his honesty, I'll sort them out. He's as honest as the day is long.' Perhaps the jockey was tempting fate by nailing his flag so firmly to the mast. In any event, he was proved dramatically wrong next time out.

It was an evening meeting at Nottingham, and just as the field was turning into the straight to approach the last three hurdles, the commentator reported: 'And there's one horse coming up the chase track.' Smarty just managed to stop Bossal before he took on the open ditch and once she knew horse and rider were safe, Jenny collapsed in laughter. John Francome, who rode the winner in the race, added a cryptic postscript. 'I don't mind him running out, Jen,' he said, 'but for a moment there I thought he was trying to get up my inner.'

Jenny Pitman's brother bought a big strapping horse called Spartacus out of Paul Cole's stable and planned to use it as a hunter. It was so well bred and so well built that Jenny persuaded him to let her train it as a prospective hurdler. Soon after Spartacus arrived, Jenny went away on holiday and when she returned she decided to ride the horse out first morning.

To her astonishment, the horse roared around the yard and then walked down the road on his hind legs. A somewhat uncomfortable Mrs Pitman yelled: 'When did this bloody thing last leave its box.' 'On Saturday morning,' said one of the lads, hesitantly. What he didn't specify was that the Saturday morning in question had been two weeks earlier.

One of the most remarkable National Hunt horses in training is Gambling Prince, a twelve-year-old gelding owned and trained by Mrs Gill Jones at Upton on Severn in Worcestershire. If Gill changed his name to 'Champion, The Wonder Horse' you could hardly claim she was exaggerating. When he's not on a racecourse Gambling Prince is used as a cattle herder on Gill's 400-acre dairy farm and rounds them up like an expert.

He's not bad on the racecourse, either. Since the late John Jones paid 310 guineas for him at the Ascot Sales in 1975 as a two-year-old who had finished tailed off in two races on the flat, Gambling Prince has never stopped winning. By the end of the 1984-5 season, the gelding had won eighteen races over hurdles and fences and collected more than £50,000 in prize money.

Gill Jones enjoys telling the story attached to his first win in the valuable Northern Hurdle at Haydock. Gambling Prince had shown promise in his first two races over hurdles at Newbury and Towcester, but he was stepping up in class at Haydock. In the paddock before the race, one established trainer looked at Gambling Prince and commented to his owner: 'Flying a bit high today, John!'

Gambling Prince proceeded to win the race by ten lengths and the following day, Ivor Herbert rang John Jones and offered him £50,000 for the horse on behalf of an American owner. The offer was refused and Gambling Prince has been flying high ever since – living proof that you can still find a bargain in racing.

Ryan Price once trained a horse called Urfe. It was owned by a Czech baron and was quite a successful hurdler. I was watching Urfe run one day at Kempton, standing near the Tattersalls' rails in the always genial company of trainer Doug Francis. As the field approached the bend into the straight, Fred Winter moved up into a challenging position on Urfe – on a tight rein.

Bookmaker Fred Binns suddenly boomed out 'What's Urfe?' And from the midst of the crowd around the bookmakers, this Cockney voice replied: 'It's sunnink they throw when you're buried, Fred.'

Speaking of dead certs, Hurst Park, pre-war, was known for the standard of lunch-time hospitality laid on for the stewards and officials. The day an old chaser called Nincompoop fell at the third last was no exception. As Nincompoop lay motionless, the vet was called for and the summons came just as the second decanter of vintage port had been finished.

The vet staggered down the course, diagnosed something serious and told the groundsman comforting Nincompoop that the horse would have to be put down. So the vet took a very unsteady aim with the humane killer – and promptly shot the groundsman through the foot. Nincompoop, meanwhile, was so alarmed by the noise and the resultant commotion that he got up and trotted off towards the stables.

Flying equally high, John McCririck, the man who's made a career out of doing tic-tac in fancy dress, was in the middle of one of his betting reports from the rails at a Sandown Park meeting on Channel 4. 'And finally Brough,' quoth McCririck, 'there are two or three horses in later races being heavily whispered around the ring – what I call psst horses . . .'

Scott, as phlegmatic as ever, took up his cue perfectly: 'Well, if we're going to have psst horses the whole thing is going to fall apart.'

IRISH

*O*ur racing scene wouldn't be half as colourful without the Irish. Great horses, brilliant trainers, superb jockeys, extrovert owners – and some crazy punters. They come in all shapes and sizes to punt and drink at Cheltenham and Liverpool. And whether they're having a fiver or five grand, they know how to get the most enjoyment from it. I'll give you two typical examples.

The scene is Cheltenham last March and two Irishman walk into the Allied Irish Bank office behind the new grandstand. 'Excuse me, miss, I'd like to withdraw £50,000 in cash, if you please,' said the first Irishman. The cashier asked him to wait while she rang Dublin and then, without batting an eyelid, returned to her desk and started counting out the money. Paddy collected his cash, waved at his friend with a satisfied flourish and said: 'Right, that's seven grand a race and we've a bit left to have a drink.'

A month later, I'm standing in the Tote queue at Liverpool to collect the returns from my each-way bet on Corbiere in the Grand National and in front of me there's this little Irish chap, proudly brandishing his ticket with a fiver each way on the winner, Last Suspect. 'That's £704, sir,' said the Tote cashier. 'How would you like it – fifties, twenties or tens?' 'I don't give a bugger how it comes, darlin',' he gasped. 'I've never had that much in me life.'

Some of the best horses in the world come out of Ireland – but going to the Emerald Isle with your cheque book can be a precarious business. I once accompanied a potential buyer to look at a three-year-old. We found him standing in a bog, and even though it was dusk we saw enough to be impressed. My owner friend, new to the game, immediately asked a price. 'Well, sir, that's difficult. How do you value such quality,' said the Irish breeder. Thinking this was the kind of business deal he clinched every day at the office, my friend suggested £8000. 'Well, let's not rush it tonight. He'll look better in the morning,' came the reply.

With that little gem of Irish logic, we were entertained regally – a marvellous meal washed down with an endless supply of Guinness. Before the black nectar began to take effect, my friend and I resolved that we had to buy the horse before nightfall – but with every glass our resolve weakened.

Sure enough, we paid the price of delay after breakfast the following morning. 'Eight grand, did you say, sir? Well last night I was tempted but I've just had a phone call from England offering me ten. You can have him for eleven – I told you he'd look better this morning.' We declined and went on our way. At our next port of call, we told another Irish breeder what had happened. 'You're well out of it,' he said. 'If that fella's horses were half as good as he reckons, they'd be twice as good as they are.'

I'm still trying to work that out.

An Irish permit-holder rang me one day and asked me to ride his horse in a novice chase at Southwell. We met in the paddock and since I'd never heard of either the trainer or the horse before, I thought I'd make a few discreet inquiries. 'What's he like, sir?' 'He's a lovely sort, to be sure . . . nice breeding . . . going like a bomb at home . . .' 'Never mind that, sir. Can he jump?' 'Beejazaj, Biddlecombe, he jumps houses!'

So I got on him, we took off and at the first we were on the floor. As I walked back, the little Irishman met me wearing that familiar look of a man who's just lost a few bob. 'What happened?' I couldn't resist it. 'Sorry, sir, he tripped over the fucking chimney pot.'

There was a three-horse race at a point-to-point in Ireland. Two horses were fancied, with the bookmakers offering evens and 5-4, and the third was a complete outsider. Just before the off, a little man with a roll of fivers could be spotted going along the front row of bookmakers, having a fiver on the outsider with each of them. Then he repeated the process as he came back along the second row. Another roll of fivers was produced and off he went on his journey through the bookmakers for a second run. By the time he reached his final port of call, there was some suspicion in the ring and the last bookmaker asked him: 'Do you know anything about this horse that we don't?' 'Nothing at all, sir,' replied the little man. 'But I do train the other two!'

Not so forthcoming was a well-known English trainer of my acquaintance. He was so secretive that if he really fancied a horse he would sleep alone in the spare room the night before the race. He was frightened he might talk in his sleep about his proposed coup, his missus would hear him and spoil the market by gossiping around the course the following day.

An Irish friend of Jenny Pitman was in the paddock at Liverpool asking about the progress as a jockey of her son Mark. At the time Jenny was trying to play down Mark's riding career so that he could complete his 'O' levels at school and go on to take his 'A' levels. 'I'm enjoying riding,' said Mark to the Irishman, 'but my mum says I've got to concentrate on my 'O' levels before I think of becoming a jockey.' If Jenny was looking for moral support from her Irish friend, it was not forthcoming. 'Oh, don't worry about it, lad. Those duckeggs will do you no good when you're coming over the last at Cheltenham.'

Irish logic, indeed. And Mark supplied some of his own shortly after he had ridden Riva Rose, trained by his mother, to an impressive win in a National Hunt flat race. A trainer asked Mark: 'Where did your Mum find that nice horse?' 'In Ireland at Ballsbridge Sales,' he replied. 'You were in the bar when she bought it.'

It was Irish 2000 Guineas Day at the Curragh and the course announcer crackled into action over the loudspeakers to welcome a large crowd. 'In just a moment I'll be giving you the alterations for the first race . . .' he said in conclusion. All over the course, racecards were taken from pockets and pens were poised. Then the Irish brogue returned to the airwaves to inform everyone: 'In the first race, they all run and the jockeys are as on the racecard.'

OWNERS

*I*t is safe to say that the most embarrassing moment of my riding career came in my last season. It was 18 December 1973, the course was Warwick and the race was the Hampton Novices Hurdle – the details are etched in indelible ink in my memory. I was riding a horse called Tammuz, trained by Fulke Walwyn and owned by Her Majesty Queen Elizabeth, the Queen Mother. I had ridden a few of the Queen Mother's horses during that season – when I was first jockey to Fulke Walwyn – but when I went to Warwick I was certain that this was going to be my first Royal winner.

My confidence looked well founded as Tammuz approached the last hurdle twenty lengths clear. This is it, I told myself, I'm going to win for the Queen Mum. But Tammuz had other ideas. He clipped the last hurdle, landed on his knees and after what seemed like an eternity of indecision – as to whether to cling on to his ears or do the sensible thing and bale out – I was on my backside on the ground.

As I sat there I said to myself: 'My God, I don't believe it. The Queen Mum's horse, a certain winner and I've fallen off the bloody thing.' If it had been possible I'd have dug a tunnel from that last hurdle, come up at the back of the stands and run. As it was I just sat there for ages – it was a horrific feeling. It helped slightly that the Queen Mother wasn't there. Sir Martin Gilliatt was her representative and he was brilliant with me. 'Don't worry, my boy, these things happen. Better luck next time,' he said.

He was right. On Boxing Day I won for the Queen Mother on Isle of Man at Kempton – despite a nasty mistake at the last – and a week later I won in a canter on Tammuz at Sandown.

Robert Sangster, the pools millionaire, is one of the cornerstones of racing in Britain and Ireland. He is one of the world's most influential owners and breeders, so you would think the last thing that enters into his calculations is superstition. Not so, it seems.

On the last day of the 1985 Chester May meeting, Mr Sangster watched three of his horses win – Seismic Wave, trained by Barry Hills won the Ormonde Stakes; Infantry, from the same stable, took the Dee Stakes; and Clanrallier, trained by Bill Watts, won a one and a half-mile handicap. A good day – even by Sangster standards.

Talking to the Press, Mr Sangster offered a remarkable explanation for his winning afternoon. 'When I looked down the list of selections in the *Birmingham Evening Mail* last night and saw that none of my horses had been tipped, I knew I had nothing to worry about,' he said. Among the assembled scribes was none other than the *Evening Mail*'s racing correspondent Ray Gilpin – a shrewd tipster on most other days and an entertaining diarist. Ray was brave enough to own up to his readers with the admission: 'I'm not completely sure what he meant, but I have a good idea!'

As someone who enters into the fray as a tipster with three selections every Saturday, I know exactly what Robert Sangster meant. I could make a living out of owners and trainers asking me not to tip their horses. And since I am a member of the Tipsters' Union, just a word or two in our defence. Tipping winners may not be so demanding physically, but in its own way it's just as hard as riding them. To all those who claim they could tip more winners than any racing correspondent, I issue a stock challenge: Tip them twenty-four hours before racing – as we have to – not a minute before the off on the racecourse or in the betting shop.

People find some weird and wonderful reasons for backing horses: a name that reminds them of their favourite aunt, the one that heeded the call of nature in the paddock, the filly with those nice red blinkers. I even know of one guy who has just one bet a day – and it's always the third horse mentioned in the column of the main tipster in his favourite national daily newspaper. He reckons that all tipsters are in league with the bookmakers and 'they' influence the nap and next best, so the third horse mentioned is the one really fancied. The theory is absolute rubbish, of course, but I tested it for seven days – and it produced five winners. I put it down to pure chance and forgot about it before my faith was eroded.

I much preferred the selection process applied by football manager Tommy Docherty when I met him at Cheltenham. Tommy's club, Wolverhampton Wanderers, were at the bottom of the Second Division at the time and hadn't scored a goal for weeks. Tommy reckoned that the 'Golden Goal' tickets at Molineux had to be reprinted and the competition renamed the 'Golden Corner'.

Tommy was perusing his racecard and couldn't make up his mind between two horses. 'I don't know whether to back Dodgy Future because it reminds me of Wolves – or Lone Raider because it reminds me of our forward line,' he said. I suggested he save his money until later and back Fast Forward – which must have reminded him of his new striker. 'You've got to be joking, Terry,' said the Doc. 'When our centre forward moves, the rest of the team know it's half-time.'

Another sports celebrity turned up one Christmas Eve, and if it hadn't been Christmas Eve, I would have sworn I was seeing things. Striding down the drive came one of my hunters – bedecked gaily with holly and tinsel and jingle bells in his main. Sitting on top, rather uncomfortably, was Father Christmas, complete with flowing red robe and long, white beard.

'Ho, ho, ho, Biddlecombe – got any nags for sale' was how my visitor introduced himself, and that one sentence had blown his cover. You don't see many Cockney Santas around Tewkesbury and I'd recognize Jimmy Greaves' voice anywhere. We've been pals for years and appear together regularly on Central Television's Friday evening sports programme. With the help of my wife, the Central lads had decided to pay me a surprise Christmas visit – but the wind-up backfired on Jimmy. He might have been without equal as a goalscorer on the football pitch, but on horseback he's a quivering wreck. Having safely negotiated the 100-yard journey from the bottom of the drive to my yard, Jimmy couldn't wait to get back on *terra firma*.

'Get me off this bloody thing, Tel,' he pleaded. 'I feel like I'm sitting on top of a skyscraper.' 'You can stay up there – and if I have any of your cheek, I'll give him a clout and you'll be off over the field.' I eventually relented, but as I was helping Jimmy dismount, my foot slipped and approximately twenty-eight stone of ex-footballer and ex-jockey were rolling in a mixture of mud and snow, covered by a Father Christmas robe.

'Bloody marvellous, ain't it,' said Jimmy. 'A lifetime on horseback and he can't even get Santa out of the saddle.'

Jimmy's next visit was more conventional and more costly. He has a great interest in horse-racing, and as I was showing him some of my young inmates, he fell in love with a three-year-old filly called Forest Track. The filly, who has a lot of presence, played her part perfectly – responding to Jimmy's every move and nuzzling her head against his while we were discussing her future. It was a match made in heaven – given even more significance by the fact that Forest Track had been bred by another former England footballer, Francis Lee. Before he realized what he'd done, Jimmy had bought her . . . but it didn't finish there.

Half an hour later Jimmy sold me a bit back and then announced: 'I'm now going to do an Arthur Daley on the lads in Central Sport and see if I can get rid of another couple of legs.' A week later a partnership was formed and Forest

Track was sent into training with Sally Oliver. I was convinced from the first day I saw her that Forest Track would win a little race either over hurdles or on the flat, and by the time you read this, either my faith will have been justified or a few of us will be deeper in debt. I hope it's the first alternative or my new owner, Mr J.P. Greaves, will never let me forget it.

Meanwhile one thought sustains me. When I met Francis Lee, now a flourishing owner-breeder and trainer in Cheshire, I told him we had bought Forest Track. 'Bad luck,' he said, 'she's useless.' Mind you, he did admit that a month after he'd sold her as a two-year-old for less than £3000, Forest Track ran at Wolverhampton and finished about a furlong in front of a horse he had paid 35,000 guineas for. We left it at that – and agreed that in racing anything can happen.

Of all the showbusiness people involved in racing as owners, Freddie Starr is one of the most enthusiastic and certainly the funniest. I went to an evening meeting at Windsor to help trainer Nan Kennedy saddle Freddie's filly Captiva as part of a feature for Central Television on the comedian's interest in horse-racing. Off-camera Freddie talks knowledgeably about racing and his string of horses, but point a lens in his direction and you are taking your life in your hands.

Central's sports reporter Bob Hall was given the task of interviewing Freddie, and if I were asked to describe his efforts in form-book language it would probably read: 'Met with interference but stayed on well.' It went something like this:

Bob (whom Freddie insisted on calling 'Paul' throughout the interview): How did you first get interested in horse-racing?

Freddie: When I was a lad, I always wanted to be a jockey but the rest of my family were all boxers – except my Dad. He was an Alsatian.

Bob: How many horses do you have?

Freddie: I've got four flat horses and all the others are round. All magnificent animals – I like them.

Bob: Do the horses like you?

Freddie: I think so. I mean, I've never actually gone up to a horse and whispered: 'Do you like me?' You get arrested for that.

Bob: What do you get out of horse-racing as an owner?

Freddie: Bills.

Bob: Do you have a bet?

Freddie: Now and again I have a little flutter – usually it's the heart. It's called punter's shake, not very good when you're holding binoculars.

Bob: What about Captiva tonight. Does she have a chance?

Freddie: It's her first time out for a year. She's got two bad legs, a dodgy hip and her neck's gone. She's wearing blinkers, a gag and a blindfold. She must have a chance.

Bob: Thanks, Mr Starr. I'll have a fiver each way.

Freddie: Thanks, Paul – and I do like that dress you're wearing.

Captiva duly ran in a six-furlong handicap and led briefly two furlongs out before finishing in the ruck. After hearing the interview, I suggested to Nan Kennedy that while the filly might be good enough to win a little race, Freddie Starr was quicker. Four months later Freddie wasn't cracking any jokes about Captiva – and the bookmakers certainly weren't laughing. The filly flew in at Warwick at 10-1 and I'm reliably informed that connections had a real touch.

Julian Belfrage, a top theatrical agent, is a keen and sporting owner who has a horse with Nick Gaselee at Lambourn called Leading Artist. The horse was a slow developer, and even as a five-year-old he would get lathered up in sweat as soon as he saw a racecourse. The first time Julian saw him on a course, Leading Artist was in the pre-parade ring and the owner didn't recognize his horse. 'I didn't think you had a runner in the race after this,' he remarked to Nick Gaselee. 'We don't,' said Nick. 'This runs in the next race – and it's yours!'

The following season at Warwick, Leading Artist was still having the same problem – and it didn't help the excitable horse when a brass band struck up next to the parade ring. Nick didn't fancy Leading Artist, but he told jockey Mark Floyd: 'Jump off and make the running – it'll give Julian a bit of a thrill seeing his horse in the lead.' Leading Artist proceeded to make all and flew in at 100-1. It was the breakthrough for the horse, who has gone on to win eight more races.

Leading Artist was the central character of a story at Towcester which proved that even Superman can be upstaged by a horse. Christopher Reeve, the Hollywood actor who flew to stardom in the *Superman* films, accompanied Julian at Towcester. Owner, trainer and everyone connected with Leading Artist recommended a bet on the horse. But Superman decided to go his own way and backed something else. Inevitably, Leading Artist trotted up.

Worcestershire owner Nick Siviter has some nice National Hunt horses in training with Sally Oliver, Martin Tate and Charlie Vernon-Miller. Every Sunday morning, Nick calls at the Oliver stable near his home to visit his horses and give a weekend treat to the likes of the useful grey County Player, who has won for him over hurdles and fences.

One Sunday, after Nick had been in the yard and had a drink with Sally and Henry Oliver, he returned to his Range Rover to find that six expensive 'Romeo y Julieta' cigars had gone missing from the parcel shelf. Only the empty tubes remained. By following a track of flaked cigar leaves, the culprit was apprehended – Sally's four-year-old son Henry John. And the brown stains around his mouth indicated that he had eaten the evidence. Henry John was suitably reprimanded and Nick now locks his Range Rover, but you can't help thinking that the lad shows early signs of good taste. After all, they were Havanas!

Alan Lee, the sports journalist who writes so expertly about racing and cricket, took me out to dinner to put together an article for the *Sporting Life* . . . and ended up buying a horse as well. Gerald Sivell had bred this nice young mare who was a half-sister to Arthur Stephenson's prolific winner Sea Merchant and he sent her to me to be broken in. The job complete, we needed to find an owner, and midway through one of Dennis Hine's excellent meals at the Corse Lawn House Hotel near my home, Alan Lee was gently persuaded to invest.

Appropriately, the mare was named Sportswords and she was put into training with my old riding pal Jeff King in Wiltshire. 'Don't worry,' I told Alan, 'she will definitely win.' And two years later Sportswords obliged in a maiden chase at Newton Abbott. She always had the stamp of a chaser, so I decided not to back her until she went over fences. Inevitably she won her first race as soon as I *stopped* backing her, following three costly unsuccessful punts.

Miss Dorothy Paget was, for many years, one of the most successful owners in both flat and National Hunt racing, but anyone who trained for her will testify that she was also one of the most demanding.

On 29 September 1948, Fulke Walwyn sent six Paget horses from his Lambourn stable to run at Folkestone. It was a memorable day for Fulke as the first five – Legal Joy, Langis Son, Jack Tatters, Endless and Loyal King – all won and, to this day, the feat is commemorated by a huge framed photograph of the successful quintet at Saxon House. The sixth runner, Loyal Monarch, was beaten by half-a-length in the last race and when the Press surrounded Miss Paget at the end of the day she was asked: 'How do you feel after an afternoon like that?' She replied: 'I'm disappointed at getting beaten in the last.'

Another determined lady owner, who was to go on and win big races with her horses, placed her first equine purchase with Derrick Candy at Wantage. After the horse had arrived at the stable, she was asked if she had any preference on racing colours. 'Oh, I don't mind what colour the jacket is,' she said. 'But I do want red breeches.'

One of the most colourful owners I ever met was Joe Sullivan, a scrap merchant on the South Coast. He had a good horse with Ryan Price called Beaver II, and you could never miss Joe on the racecourse because of his loud, infectious laugh. He would buy and sell anything at a profit. He once bought a crumbling sea wall, broke it up at his yard and sold it as hard core. Joe was also a devilish practical joker – and Josh Gifford and 'Buck' Jones fell hook, line and sinker for his best wind-up.

Josh, Buck and Paul Kellaway were all with Ryan Price at Findon and shared a cottage. The telephone rang one day and it was Joe Sullivan, inviting all three of them to a 'big party' at a pub in deepest Kent. 'Be there at eight o'clock, we'll have a great night,' said Joe, and gave explicit instructions on how to reach the pub. Paul had to decline because of a previous commitment, but Josh and Buck – knowing the standard of Joe's hospitality – couldn't wait to get there.

It took them a two-hour drive to reach their destination, and it turned out to be a little old country pub which didn't look too lively. They parked the car in the deserted car park and ran through pouring rain to reach the bar. Inside they found just one person – the publican, sitting behind the bar with his pipe and a pint. 'Where's the party?' asked Josh. 'Party? There's no party here.' 'But there has to be – we were given the name of your pub.' 'You must be joking – nobody ever comes here on a night like this.'

To make matters worse – and Paul Kellaway is normally in tears when we reach this stage of the story – Josh and Buck had two flat tyres when they went back to the car to begin the long journey home. The following morning Joe Sullivan rang them and asked: 'Did you enjoy the party?'

One of Jenny Pitman's owners accompanied her to Ballsbridge Sales near Dublin. He's known as a very bluff Yorkshireman who likes his pints of beer with a whiskey chaser and like most visitors to Ballsbridge he rarely had an empty glass. The owner fancied a filly which had passed through the ring and asked Jenny to take a look at the horse in her stall. The animal turned out to be a real madam. As soon as the stall was opened, she flew at her visitors, ears pinned back. Then the filly whipped round and relieved herself – all over Jenny's new white mack.

The Yorkshireman, standing a pace back, thought it was hilarious and still dines out on the story of how Jenny got peed on. What he doesn't know is the tail end of the incident. While he fell about laughing at Jenny, the filly's offerings also landed in his pint of beer – and he drank the lot of it!

A Polish businessman rang Jenny Pitman one day and asked her to accompany him to Ascot Sales to buy a horse. The stable had runners at two meetings, so neither Jenny nor her assistant trainer David Stait were able to go to the sales. 'I'll go and buy one myself,' suggested the Pole. 'Don't do that; you won't know what you're buying,' said Jenny, and recommended a bloodstock agent who was available to advise him.

That evening, Jenny and David returned from racing and saw a new head sticking out of one of their boxes. 'Pretty filly,' said Jenny, but when she walked into the box for a closer look she concluded: 'She's got about as much bone as my labrador.' The Polish owner had selected the filly himself, paid about £400 and indicated to Jenny that she might win the Oaks.

The problem for Jenny didn't end there. As soon as she started training the filly, she discovered that her new charge had desperately sore shins – so bad that some mornings the filly couldn't even get out of her box. Jenny eventually told the owner: 'I know she's got a pretty head, but she's not going to do the job. Either take her home and turn her out or get rid of her.' The owner replied: 'I used to be a runner and I sometimes suffered from sore shins. I got rid of the problem by soaking my shins in a Radox bath. Can't you try that with the filly?' 'Well, I could,' said Jenny, rapidly losing patience, 'but I'd have a bloody job getting her upstairs to the bathroom.'

For many years Jack Taylor was Britain's top soccer referee – an official of international repute who reached the pinnacle of his career when he took charge of the 1974 World Cup Final between West Germany and Holland. But these days you are more likely to see Jack at the racecourse rather than the football ground. He is the keenest of owners and has horses in training with Bill Preece in Shropshire. Jack tells some lovely stories about his experiences as a referee – including a gem against himself.

Denis Law, the great Scotland international, had a reputation for trying to cajole referees into making decisions in his team's favour, and during one game Jack decided to put him in his place. After about half-an-hour of chat from Denis, Jack halted play, called him over and asked: 'Who's refereeing this game, Denis – you or me?' 'At the moment, Jack,' replied Denis, 'neither of us.'

But it was Jack Taylor who came out on top when we were discussing the future of two racehorses – his newly acquired hurdler Mitilini and Forest Track, the filly I have a share in. 'We'll probably come across each other in a race soon,' said I. 'We'll have to have a small side-stake.' 'I can't see that happening, Terry,' said Jack. 'We don't plan to run ours in sellers.'

Postcript

My most unusual venture into ownership concerned a racing pigeon.

Duggie Wellon, a good pal and near-neighbour in Gloucestershire, is an expert with racing pigeons and has some top-class birds in his 'stable'. He invited me to become joint-owner of one well-bred bird whom we decided to call Arkle. Duggie brought the bird to show me – as proud as any racehorse breeder with a high-class yearling. I looked at it and was not impressed. For a start, it seemed to have a club foot. 'Don't worry about that, Terry,' said my pal, 'he doesn't fly with his feet.'

So Duggie trained Arkle, and although another pal of mine suggested we should fit a clockwork motor and wind him up, the pigeon began to show a bit of form. We sent him for a race from the South Coast and he came home in his own time. He didn't trouble the judge, but he was hardly tailed off. What this bird needs, we decided, is a trip. He was more of a four-mile chaser than a five-furlong sprinter, so Duggie got him trained to the minute and we entered him in a race from Nantes in France to Gloucester.

We were already counting our money when Arkle was despatched across the Channel. That was eighteen months ago. We haven't seen him since.

AND FINALLY

F inally, an admission. I have to own up to taking part in a fixed race. It was in the summer of 1985 – on Derby Day to be precise and while the nation's attention was focused on Epsom, there was a fix in Herefordshire.

The venue was Almley Races, one of the most popular centres for the growing sport of harness racing, and I was making my first appearance as a driver. It was all in good fun, of course, because we were filming a feature on the trotting for Central Television's sports programme. Even the bookies entered into the spirit of things and laid a mock 4-1 against me winning the race.

I was driving Jolene, a fast filly owned and trained by Ted Phillips from Powys, and we took on a field of five over one mile and 134 yards. The idea was that I would ride a waiting race and then on the last circuit move into the lead before holding off a late challenge from one of harness racing's top partnerships, Tom Harper and Temple Star.

The best-laid plans almost went astray. I had never driven a sulky in a race before and after only two practice laps, I was a bit green. When you've spent most of your life on top of a horse, it's a strange feeling to be behind one on wheels and I did have my problems. On the first lap, a horse behind me took a bite at my shoulder, and when it was time to go into the lead I was squeezed for room, despite the kind efforts of the other drivers.

I've never been one to resist a chance to go up the inner. This time, however, I forgot that I had to get the wheels through as well as the horse – and we missed a collision with a rather sturdy marker post by about a quarter-of-an-inch. Having accomplished this, the race was mine and I won by a diminishing half-a-length, thanks to Tom Harper managing to 'strangle' Temple Star all the way up the straight. Fixed it may have been, but the 906th winner of my career gave me as much pleasure as many of the others.